DATE DUE

Brodart Co.   Cat. # 55 137 001   Printed in USA

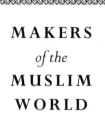

MAKERS
of the
MUSLIM
WORLD

Ahmad al-Mansur

SELECTION OF TITLES IN THE MAKERS OF THE MUSLIM WORLD SERIES

Series editor: Patricia Crone,
Institute for Advanced Study, Princeton

For current information and details of other books in the series, please visit www.oneworld-publications.com

MAKERS
of the
MUSLIM
WORLD

Ahmad al-Mansur

The Beginnings of Modern Morocco

MERCEDES GARCÍA-ARENAL

ONEWORLD

OXFORD

A Oneworld Book

Published by Oneworld Publications 2009

Copyright © Mercedes García-Arenal 2009

ISBN 978–1–85168–610–0

Typeset by Jayvee, Trivandrum, India
Printed and bound in India for Imprint Digital

Oneworld Publications
185 Banbury Road
Oxford OX2 7AR
England
www.oneworld-publications.com

CONTENTS

ACKNOWLEDGMENTS

I have enjoyed writing this book very much. It has enabled me to assemble, revise, complete and interpret anew much of what I have been working on for so many years. I wish to offer my heartfelt thanks to Patricia Crone, the editor of *Makers of the Muslim World*, for allowing me to write it, as well as for her careful reading and critical comments. The report of the Oneworld external referee was also extremely useful.

I owe a great debt to Martin Beagles and to Heather Ecker, thanks to whom this book is in idiomatic English. Their comments and suggestions have been a great help and have improved the text in many ways, not only linguistic. I am grateful for their help in transmitting the fascination I feel for Ahmad al-Mansur and his world and the enjoyment I have derived from writing about him, which I hope is apparent in the text.

My thanks are due to Scotford Lawrence, who showed me the portrait of Abd al-Wahid, the Moroccan ambassador to England, and put me in touch with the curator's office at Birmingham University, which has permitted its reproduction here. My colleagues at the Consejo Superior de Investigaciones Científicas (CSIC) in Madrid, Maribel Fierro (another author in this series) and Fernando R. Mediano, read the whole manuscript and made valuable suggestions and critical remarks, as did my friend and colleague Roy Foster and my husband Gonzalo Gil – the latter two 'outsiders' to the field of Arabic and Islamic studies, who made me expand and explain as well as correct and clarify. My daughter Clara has been very agreeable in letting me talk to her about Ahmad for more than a year, asking unexpected questions and helping me in many ways.

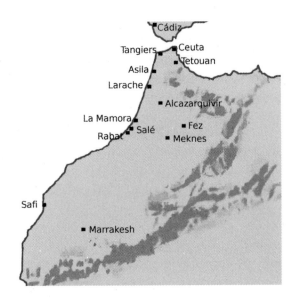

Morocco in the time of Ahmad al-Mansur

INTRODUCTION

The well-known Orientalist Bernard Lewis (*The Muslim Discovery of Europe*, London, 1982, p. 118) described early modern Morocco in the following terms: 'In the world of Islam, Morocco, in Arabic called al-Maghrib al-Aqsà, the Far West, was a remote and isolated outpost and a comparatively small and weak country at that.' Morocco was remote from the main power centres of the Middle East, and remains remote to the interests of most scholars of the Islamic world today. However, during the age of Sultan Muley Ahmad al-Mansur, Morocco was neither small nor weak – not at least in the mind of the sultan himself, nor in the opinions of the Ottoman sultan Murat III, Queen Elizabeth I of England, Philip II of Spain or the Dutch *stadhouder*. During the course of a reign that lasted almost a quarter of a century (1578–1603), Ahmad al-Mansur brought Morocco to the forefront of international politics and subjected it to a process of modernization, to bring it up-to-date with Ottoman Turkey and with Europe. Morocco's commercial and economic success under al-Mansur did not go unnoticed by his contemporaries abroad. Thus, the Spanish Duke of Medinasidonia (who was to lead the Armada to defeat against the English in 1588), a leading expert in Moroccan affairs, wrote to Philip II in 1584: 'Barbary is no longer what it was, for in it are wealth and curiosity.' Wealth and curiosity were important traits found in Ahmad al-Mansur himself. To these one might add ambition: his most grandiose aim was to become an emperor after the fashion of Philip of Spain or the Ottoman Murat. Ahmad al-Mansur presided over the beginnings of modern Morocco, and thus finds his place in the series *Makers of the Muslim World*.

Lewis's 'remote and isolated outpost' evokes Morocco as a country closed in upon itself, impenetrable to Europeans (until the period of French and Spanish colonization), impermeable to its northern neighbours and cut off from its neighbours to the east. Whatever the reality of Morocco's isolation today, if it is still perceived as remote, hindsight provides us with a very different view.

In fact, the Morocco of Muley Ahmad al-Mansur was very much connected with the world of its time and that is what being 'modern' means. It partook in international politics and diplomacy, in trade, in conquest and in discovery. As an example, we can choose a single year: in 1593, in the middle of al-Mansur's reign, an embassy from the Western Sudan brought an elephant to Marrakesh that made a tremendous impression on the population of the city. Its impact was similar to that caused by Hanno, the white elephant brought from India to Rome a few decades earlier as a gift to Pope Leo X from the King of Portugal, Don Manuel. The possession of exotic animals was a sign of the greatness of emperors, an emblem of their influence over remote regions where exotic animals roamed wild. Not so long before, Ahmad al-Mansur had asked Philip II to send him an artist to paint his portrait, another sign of royalty. In the same city of Marrakesh that year of 1593, legal scholars argued whether the new substance known as tobacco was apt for legitimate consumption or was unlawful. The new royal palace, al-Badi', was being built by the Sultan, for which he had brought the best foreign architects and artisans to Marrakesh. The marble for the palace was imported from Italy. This marble had been bought with Moroccan sugar, weight for weight. Moroccan sugar was so superior that Queen Elizabeth of England refused to use any other in her household. In 1589, Queen Elizabeth consumed 18,000 pounds of sugar, paid for at 14 pence a pound. Ahmad al-Mansur proposed a joint venture to the English Queen to conquer the Spanish territories in America. His plan was not very different from the one proposed ten years earlier by Francis Drake for the conquest of Peru, a plan that forced the Spaniards – well informed by their spies – to fortify the port of Callao on the Pacific coast. In 1591, Ahmad al-Mansur launched an expedition across the Sahara to conquer the Songhay kingdom of Gao and Timbuktu to search for sources of gold, much like the Spanish conquistadors, or Sir Walter Raleigh in his search for El Dorado. There is no question that Muley Ahmad al-Mansur was very much a ruler of his time.

Morocco's physical location between three great regions of communication and trade, the Atlantic Ocean, the Mediterranean Sea and the Saharan desert, and its political location between the dominant powers of the sixteenth century – the Spanish Habsburgs and the Ottoman Turks – made it a country of great strategic importance. Morocco also represented a frontier territory between Europe and the Islamic World. It was a borderland that absorbed peoples expelled from the Iberian Peninsula, such as the Jews and Muslims of Granada, and integrated them as technicians, merchants and consultants to the administration. It was a country that sought to imitate the political powers it admired – the Ottoman, Spanish and British Empires – and to borrow from them elements that the sultan believed had brought about the wealth and power of those nations. Morocco was a country that played a leading role in the international politics of the sixteenth century, forming alliances with Christian nations when faced with rivals at home or the threat of force from other Islamic powers.

In the rivalry between Turks and Spaniards for control of the Mediterranean, Morocco played a fundamental role: Ahmad al-Mansur learned how to bend the rivalry to his advantage. He also learned how to profit from the division between Catholic and Protestant Europe, a division that gave Ahmad al-Mansur room to manoeuvre. While it is true that events external to Morocco contributed greatly to his importance in international politics, al-Mansur saw how to make weaknesses opportunities.

The country's main sources of weakness were the Iberian colonies on Moroccan soil, established in the late fifteenth century. At that time, Spain and Portugal had divided up the world between them, and Morocco was subjected to what might be described as an extension of the peninsular process of the so-called *Reconquista*. Thus, Mediterranean ports such as Melilla fell under Spanish control, as did Tlemcen for a time, and most importantly Oran, on Morocco's eastern border. During the fifteenth century, the Portuguese succeeded in conquering most of Morocco's Atlantic ports, from Tangier and Ceuta, down the coast to Agadir, making access to the sea impossible for the Moroccans themselves, who were reduced to using a handful of small ports: Rabat-Salé, Larache and Tetouan. Although by the second half of the sixteenth century all ports down the Atlantic coast except Mazagan/al-Jadida had been lost or evacuated by the Portuguese, Morocco still found it difficult to participate in international trade and was prevented from having its own navy. Instead, the Moroccan-controlled ports of the Atlantic coast became much-feared centres of operations against Spanish ships sailing out to the East and West Indies or returning to Europe with rich cargoes of spices, silks or precious metals. Pirates of all nationalities created shelters and supply havens on the Moroccan coast, and as a result Spain developed an interest in creating its own points of support in the region.

Despite the process of almost colonial advance – or perhaps precisely because of it – Ahmad al-Mansur's ambition was to achieve supremacy over the lands of Islam to which he felt he was more entitled than the Ottoman sultan. He wanted symbolic as well as political power. Thus, he undertook a series of reforms in his public administration and the armed forces to set about building an empire of his own. His army crossed the Sahara to conquer the Western Sudan. At the same time, he entertained hopes that Elizabeth I would allow him to assist her in a conquest of the Spanish American territories or southern Spain, or alternatively that an alliance with Spain might permit him to wrest the regencies of Algiers and Tunis from Ottoman control. Al-Mansur also undertook sophisticated propaganda campaigns and established an elaborate court ceremonial. As part of the same programme, he built up a monumental capital, Marrakesh, that served as a stage for the projection of his absolute, universalizing dominance to his own subjects, to Muslims in general and to Europeans.

Vis-à-vis his subjects, Ahmad al-Mansur felt entitled to his position, as he was a *sharif*, or descendant of the Prophet Muhammad.

That is what his title Muley ('my lord') means. His membership of the holiest of all lineages conferred upon him the kind of charisma and religious authority that legitimized his possession of absolute political power. In the eyes both of his own subjects and of foreign observers, his authority was confirmed by his near-miraculous and completely unexpected rise to power in 1578 as a result of the battle of Alcazar. In it, he won a resounding victory over the army of King Don Sebastian of Portugal, who had launched a military expedition to conquer Morocco – hence his title Al-Mansur, 'The Victorious'.

The young Portuguese king, who had no heirs, died during the battle. It was a catastrophic venture for Portugal, which lost its independence as a result. Philip II of Spain, son of a Portuguese princess, inherited the throne of Portugal and united both crowns under his command, in the so-called 'Iberian union'. The battle of Alcazar, described by historian Fernand Braudel as 'Mediterranean Christianity's last Crusade', was an event that also produced consternation in England, France and Holland.

It is thanks to this battle that Ahmad made his first appearance in the historical record, and it is only then that his biography can truly begin – or rather only then that the sources give us the first scraps with which a biography can be constructed. It was this battle that made Europeans become aware of the existence of a man called Muley Ahmad al-Mansur.

THE BATTLE OF ALCAZAR

The battle of Alcazar in 1578 had a stunning effect on the whole of Europe. In Portugal, a long time passed before the topic could even be broached. At first, there were only rumours that no one was willing to confirm. News arrived slowly, as unacceptable and intolerable stories. It would be years before the defeated could bring themselves to write chronicles or accounts of the battle, and many more before such accounts would be published.

In Morocco, on the winning side, the surprise and amazement were so great that the victory was not followed up as it might have been. Victory at Alcazar might have led to the recovery of the Moroccan ports under Portuguese control, but the relief felt at the danger that had been averted was considered sufficient. In fact, victory over the mammoth Portuguese army was such an unexpected event that it could only be interpreted as being due to divine intervention. The sheer size of the armies on that morning of 4 August 1578 was extraordinary. In the blazing heat of a plain in north-western Morocco, beside the Wadi-l-Makhazin (this tributary of the river Lukus was near to the small town of Alcazar, after which the conflict was named), were some twenty-six thousand men on the Portuguese side, led by their young king, Don Sebastian. His pretext for invading Morocco had been the defence of a candidate to the Moroccan throne, Muhammad al-Mutawakkil, nephew of the reigning sultan, who brought with him three thousand of his own followers. Against him stood the reigning sultan of Morocco, Abd al-Malik, with a force of more than thirty thousand men. An immense battle took place, involving nearly sixty thousand soldiers, proportions hitherto known only in warfare at sea.

The battle became known as the 'Battle of the Three Kings' because three kings lost their lives in it; this fact alone gave it a quasi-mythological dimension. Don Sebastian died in action on the battle-field itself. Muhammad al-Mutawakkil drowned in the river Wadi-l-Makhazin while retreating, swept away by tidal waters fast enough to sweep him off his horse. When his body was discovered, it was flayed, stuffed with straw and displayed throughout Morocco. Abd al-Malik, the reigning sultan, who was already seriously ill at the start of the battle – possibly with the plague – died on his litter as the fighting raged, although his death was kept secret until the encounter was over. Ahmad, Abd al-Malik's virtually unknown younger brother and his deputy in the battle, inherited the throne and was to reap the glory and prestige brought by the famous victory. Dramatically, Ahmad was named sultan on the battlefield itself, where the army hierarchies swore homage and fealty to the new king.

Don Sebastian, King of Portugal – one of the leading world pow-ers of the day and the centre of an empire stretching from Goa in India as far as Brazil – died heirless, and almost all of his nobles died or were captured at the battle of Alcazar. Virtually all of the Portuguese nobility, among males, was wiped out, including military officials: in all, twelve thousand young men lost their lives, and fourteen thousand were captured. An Arab chronicler from the court of Ahmad al-Mansur wrote at the time, not without sarcasm, that the bishops of Portugal had been forced to consider the possibility of sanctioning polygamy, so scarce was the number of men left.

The Portuguese crown was inherited by the dead king's great-uncle, Cardinal Don Henrique, over seventy years old, and feeble of mind and body. One year later he died as well, and the Portuguese court in Tomar decided to accept as heir to the throne another of Don Sebastian's uncles, Philip II of Spain. Philip united the two empires in 1580 and Portugal ceased to be an independent nation for sixty years. Philip was able to use silver from America to ransom the Portuguese captives in Morocco, but the battle was an unqualified tragedy for Portugal, and an event with tremendous implications for the whole of Europe.

WHY DID THE BATTLE TAKE PLACE?

Don Sebastian's involvement had been brought about, in principle, by an appeal from one of the two sides in a Moroccan dynastic dispute; the brothers of the deceased sultan had confronted that sultan's sons in a struggle for the throne. Although the details of such disputes can make for tedious narrative, and often include the brief appearance of secondary figures with unpronounceable names who later disappear from view, the technicalities are important in this case.

The dynasty concerned was the Sa'dian dynasty, which had assumed control in Morocco in the mid-sixteenth century. The Sa'dian family originally came from the south of the country, from a region between the foothills of the Atlas Mountains and the desert known as the Sus. Its members defended their right to be known as *sharifs*, descendants of the Prophet Muhammad through his daughter Fatima. Chroniclers of the dynasty make use of a well-known and much-repeated topos in western Arabic literature to explain its origins: a group of inhabitants of the oases to the south of the Atlas, after suffering a series of poor harvests, travelled to the Arabian peninsula in search of a *sharif* willing to return with them to their land and settle among them, so that his *baraka* or charisma would cause their land to flourish again. This kind of mythical account linked the prestige attached to all that came from the Middle East – the cradle of Islam – with the sacred lineage and thaumaturgical power of the family concerned. The members of the family, the Banu Sa'd or Sa'dians, showed clear signs of combative holiness. They reformed the customs of the primitive Berber tribes of the south in accordance with the law. They also preached armed struggle against the Portuguese occupants of the coastal ports and their allies, the Arabs of the Atlantic plains close to those ports, and also encouraged the use of arms against the ruling dynasty of Fez, the Wattasids, that had made pacts with both. The Wattasids were, in the view of the Sa'dians, corrupt and ineffective in their defence of Islam and the Muslims.

The Banu Sa'd received the support of the Sufi religious brotherhoods (discussed in the next chapter), which held an extraordinary amount of power and influence in rural areas and helped provide the Sa'dians with a quasi-messianic form of propaganda. Sufi support was decisive in the triumph of the founder of the dynasty, Muhammad al-Shaykh al-Sa'di, who took the title *al-Qaim bi-Amr Allah*, 'he who executes God's order, he who does what God says must be done', a title appropriate for a *Mahdi*, or Islamic messiah. Muhammad al-Shaykh defeated the Portuguese in control of the port of Santa Cruz do Cabo do Gue (Agadir), and expelled them from it. Years later, in 1549, he was able to conquer Fez and bring down its reigning dynasty. This defeat was seen as an alarming development not only by Spain and Portugal but also by the Turks, who sought to extend their sovereignty over the only remaining independent Muslim country in the Mediterranean. None of the three empires was pleased to see Morocco gaining strength, and in 1557 Muhammad al-Shaykh was assassinated in Fez by members of his Turkish guard acting upon instructions from Istanbul.

Muhammad's death brought two principles of succession into direct conflict. On the one hand, there was the principle that the heir should be the eldest son of the deceased ruler. Contrary to this, there was another notion, that the ruler's successor should be the eldest male member of the family. First, Abdallah, Muhammad's eldest son, was crowned in Fez just hours after his father's death. The new sultan immediately ordered the execution of all those brothers and nephews who had not moved quickly enough to reach places of safety. Though brutal, Abdallah's actions were an efficient means of preventing rivalries, a strategy adopted by his near-contemporaries Suleyman the Magnificent in Istanbul and Ivan the Terrible in Russia. Both had rid themselves of relatives and possible rivals. However, Abdallah was not quite as efficient as Suleyman or Ivan, and three of his brothers escaped: Abd al-Mu'min, Abd al-Malik – the sultan who died later at the battle of Alcazar – and Ahmad, the subject of this study, who was at that time still a young boy. The three brothers took refuge with their retinues and their mothers in Tlemcen, then in the Turkish territory of Algiers, and moved from there to Istanbul, where they lived until the death of their older brother Abdallah. Abdallah was succeeded, in accordance with his wishes, by his eldest son, Muhammad al-Mutawakkil, who came to the throne in 1574.

That year, the new sultan's uncle, Abd al-Malik, returned to Morocco with the aid of a Turkish army sanctioned and supported by Istanbul. This marked the beginning of a civil war between uncle and nephew that lasted for some two years. In the battle that resolved the matter in Abd al-Malik's favour, victory was determined by the fact that his ranks were swelled by 'Andalusian' soldiers – immigrants from al-Andalus, originally Muslims from the Iberian Peninsula (we will return to the Andalusians and their motives for favouring the candidate supported by the Turks in due course). Muhammad, the dethroned sultan, fled with a group of followers and armed men, first to the Rock or Peñón de Vélez de la Gomera, one of the Moroccan ports that had been conquered by Spain. Once there, he sent a delegation to Philip II asking for assistance to recover his throne. Such aid, whether Turkish or Spanish, was never given for naught: both countries sought to extend their influence in Moroccan affairs, and both had designs on Larache, an Atlantic port of great strategic importance, and one of the most important in Moroccan hands. Philip II wanted it to defend Spanish ships returning from America and the southern coasts of the Peninsula from attacks by corsairs. The Turks aimed to extend their sovereignty as far as the Atlantic and were attempting to recover their influence over the Western Mediterranean after the defeat of Lepanto in 1571.

But on this occasion Philip II refused to help Muhammad, because he had already established diplomatic relations with the new ruler, his uncle Abd al-Malik. When he did not receive the answer he had expected from Spain, Muhammad went to the Portuguese territory of Tangier and sent off another delegation, this time to Don Sebastian of Portugal. Muhammad offered Sebastian the port of Asila in exchange for the military aid necessary to recover his throne. Don

Sebastian, who already had plans to invade Morocco, received his request with great enthusiasm.

It may seem surprising that a candidate to the throne of Morocco should request assistance from the two Catholic Iberian nations, especially in the light of the anti-Christian propaganda that had helped the Sa'adian family come to power and of the ideology that family employed subsequently. However, the projection of oneself as leader of the *jihad* was a propagandistic leitmotiv that rarely had any practical application, and only served to confer legitimacy on a dynasty's military actions and fiscal impositions. And there was precedent. Alliances between Christian kings and Andalusian and Moroccan sovereigns were formed during the last two centuries of the *Reconquista* of the Iberian Peninsula. During that period, Castilian involvement in the internal affairs of the Islamic dynasty of Granada was constant. Castilian kings would support one or another candidate or rival, and gave shelter at court to those who were defeated in internal disputes, or to noblemen who had fallen into disgrace. Likewise, Castilian rebels or rivals would turn to Granada for assistance in times of civil war, and take shelter at the court of its Nasrid sultan when necessary. These alliances were, then, a custom deriving from the final phase of the *Reconquista*, and were characteristic of the frontier.

One of the main features of Muslim Spain (al-Andalus) throughout its history is that it *was* a frontier, a moving, changing, porous frontier where negotiation was necessary and mutual influence was unavoidable. Both Christian and Muslim portions of Spain were constantly divided by internal conflicts during the medieval period. Both territories were defined by adherence to a faith considered by its followers to be superior and exclusive. But, when a religious or ideological movement under unified political command was torn by internal dissension, conflict with the opposing faith became less important than the struggle within the same faith. This is a well-known phenomenon that explains why rival factions in al-Andalus or the Christian territories sometimes preferred to forge alliances with others of a different faith in order to wage war on their co-religionists.

When al-Andalus disappeared, Morocco took its place as the frontier territory, the border with Iberian Christianity having shifted south. As such, it became the scene of many of the phenomena that for centuries had occurred on the northern side of the Strait of Gibraltar. Despite their feelings of mutual distrust, and despite all official discourse, both the Christians of Iberia and the Muslims of Morocco regarded alliances with the Infidel as a minor evil to be resorted to when confronted with powerful enemies.

THE MAIN PROTAGONISTS AT THE BATTLE OF ALCAZAR

Don Sebastian

Don Sebastian was, in many ways, a medieval king, a figure not of his own time. In 1578, he was a solitary young man of twenty-four, filled with knightly ideals more appropriate to a previous age, a man with an ardent and combative faith obsessed with crusading ideals. Since he was a boy, Sebastian had showed a keen interest in arms and tales of military endeavours. He was the grandson and successor of the great king Don João III, whose sons died young except for Sebastian's father, who married Philip II's sister. Sebastian's father died a few weeks before the birth of his son, and after the birth his mother left him in the care of her mother-in-law, Queen Catalina, widow of João III, and returned to Spain. The young Sebastian was brought up by his grandmother and his great-uncle, Cardinal Don Henrique, until Catalina's death in 1568, when Sebastian ascended the Portuguese throne at the age of fourteen. He had been raised in a deeply religious atmosphere, surrounded by elderly relatives in a court saddened and overshadowed by the death of so many family members. Educated in the love of God and in knightly arts, he was so taken by both that he rejected all attempts to make him consider marriage.

Don Sebastian dreamed of conquering Morocco and converting infidels to the true faith. He saw the plea for assistance from the dethroned Muley Muhammad as an ideal opportunity to fulfil his ambitions. The Portuguese Empire, like the Spanish, had been built on the foundations of a messianic and providential ideology that aspired, ultimately, to conquer Jerusalem, unite all humanity under the same Law and Shepherd, and restore throughout the world the primitive purity of the early Church. These medieval ideals of a Last Emperor were, in the case of the Portuguese, linked to the dream of conquering Fez – a city with a rich presence in eschatological myths – and the conquest of Jerusalem.

Don Sebastian received Muley Muhammad's plea for help with enthusiasm, but his advisers remained unconvinced and did not support the plan to chase after a Moroccan chimera. His great-uncle and tutor, the elderly Cardinal Don Henrique, his uncle, Philip II of Spain, and the main noblemen at court spoke unanimously against the adventure and tried to dissuade him from embarking upon it. But their efforts were in vain. Philip II sent his well-known courtier, the soldier and poet Francisco de Aldana, to Morocco, disguised as a Jew, to gather information about Moroccan armies and fortifications. He was instructed to write a memoir that exaggerated the obstacles so as to dissuade Don Sebastian from his plan. Aldana remained in Morocco for three months, mainly in Fez, but instead of writing against the Moroccan expedition, he became one of its main supporters: he wrote the famous *Octavas* for Don Sebastian in which he alerted him to many threats that required his action. The *Octavas* is a bellicose poem in which Iberia is besieged by various enemies. The principal enemies are the Turks – on the verge of arriving at the Atlantic shore – who would sail with the Moroccans to the West Indies and vanquish the Spanish there. Aldana accompanied Don Sebastian to Alcazar and died with him during the battle. That a Spaniard who spoke only Spanish and Italian, disguised as a Jew, could live and travel in Morocco without raising suspicions is an interesting fact to which I shall come back.

Don Sebastian commanded all of his noblemen to join him and to recruit troops from their localities. He ordered proclamations to be trumpeted throughout Portugal that any nobleman, gentleman or *hidalgo* who refused to participate in the invasion with all of his men would automatically lose his land, rents and privileges. The leading noblemen duly arrived with farmworkers and peasant draftees who scarcely knew how to hold a weapon. Portuguese children between the ages of eight and eleven were among the captives later taken at the battle of Alcazar. Faced with the reticence of Spain, which was only prepared to lend him two thousand men with the condition that such assistance would be given only if the adventure was limited to restoring Muhammad to the throne and conquering the port of Larache, Don Sebastian was forced to recruit German mercenaries. He also borrowed men from other forces, like those commanded by the Irish mercenary and pirate Thomas Stukely, who in early 1578 happened to find himself in the port of Lisbon with a group of six hundred men given to him by Pope Gregory XIII to assist Irish Catholic rebels in their struggles with the English. Don Sebastian invited Stukely – who had fought alongside Philip II at Lepanto – to join his mission, and the Irishman's highly undisciplined soldiers joined Sebastian's invading force, along with whatever problems they were to cause later.

In fact, the adventure was troubled even before the troops left Lisbon. Preparations were drawn out and ineffective, and the whole of Portugal was subjected to religious processions and rogations in an atmosphere of fervour and impending doom. Sebastian commanded every ship in every port of his kingdom to be brought to Lisbon, and gradually built up supplies of foodstuffs and other equipment. Throughout the long process of preparation, Philip II continued to warn against the project, ordering the Duke of Alba – well-known for his bloody repression of Flanders and certainly not a man to be accused of squeamishness – to draw up a written report expounding on the absurdity of the mission. Portuguese noblemen knelt before the king, telling him that if it was his wish to see their throats cut, he should order it then and there, in Portugal. Finally, the Duke of Medinasidonia tried to persuade the young king that even if the adventure went ahead, Sebastian himself should remain at home in Portugal. But the objections fell on deaf ears.

Juan de Silva, the Spanish ambassador to Lisbon, makes it clear in his extraordinary letters to Philip II in the spring of 1578 that Don Sebastian was overwhelmed with excitement and enthusiasm for his project. Silva recorded for Philip minute details of Sebastian's conduct, writing that his excitement could be noted in his manner and way of dressing: 'the king is very fresh and healthy, dressed in colours and with many feathers, which he was never wont to use'. The Portuguese noblemen, on the other hand, were described as 'sad and angry'. They had good cause.

Six hundred ships finally left Lisbon on the Day of St John, 24 June 1578. It was the very worst time of the year to be travelling south to fight battles in Africa, and even before the ships had left Lisbon the health of many of the German mercenaries was affected by the heat. To make matters worse, the voyage was prolonged by Sebastian's determination to create a spectacle. As they passed the southern Spanish city of Cadiz, tournaments and bullfights were organized on the shore so that the Portuguese king could view them from his brigantine. Juan de Silva, who continued to accompany the expedition, expressed his surprise that the king, under the circumstances, should entertain himself with 'such childish things'. At the same time, it was useful to please him 'so that he does not complain that we are not helping him'.

Indeed, Don Sebastian was quite pleased: he believed that he would generate fear in Africa, and he carried with him a crown of gold with which to declare himself 'Emperor of Morocco' after the conquest, as well as rich clothing and packsaddles for his personal guard that bore the royal arms and dynastic insignia. His chaplain had prepared a victory sermon, and carried it with him amongst his belongings.

The Portuguese force arrived in Tangier in July, where it joined up with Muhammad al-Mutawakkil and his followers. Together they proceeded towards Asila, the port recently sacrificed to the Portuguese and which, a few years later, Philip II would return to Ahmad al-Mansur. At Asila, at the end of the month, the true seriousness of the situation began to become clear: the troops lacked food, there was frequent squabbling among the soldiers (especially between the Germans and Italians), the heat was making itself felt and a large number of soldiers fell ill. Dysentery and other epidemics became more widespread by the day, and the news brought by spies in Morocco was far from encouraging, telling of a powerful and well-organized Moroccan army waiting inland.

Some of the leading members of the expedition, the Count of Vimioso, the Bishop of Coimbra and others with military experience, went to speak to the king and told him, with great affection and kind words, that he had to be strong and hold back rather than advance towards certain defeat in open country. Sebastian simply laughed at them and called them 'Jews'. What did he mean by such an epithet? Clearly, it was intended as an insult, but what exactly did it convey? Perhaps that his advisers were men of little valour or honour, who made calculations and thought only in terms of their own gain, all qualities ascribed to Jews by ugly contemporary stereotypes. But in this insult lies a better explanation as to why the Portuguese nobility followed the king against their better judgement, without ever attempting mutiny, and finally rendered the ultimate sacrifice, a subject of much commentary at the time. They did so in order to demonstrate that they were honourable men of noble origin and of 'clean blood' that was untainted by Moorish or Jewish ancestors, of a lineage that gave them a right to privilege. For an inhabitant of Iberia during the sixteenth century, to have 'clean blood' was more important than life itself, because of its implications for future generations. The strength of this idea and its implications say much about the kind of power that could be exercised by an absolute monarch at the beginning of the modern age in a society that still retained feudal characteristics.

The army set off towards Alcazar on 1 August. For four days, it moved slowly, as the heavily armoured riders had to cope with unbearable heat, virtually no water and drastically reduced rations. The cannons were pulled by oxen. On the morning of 4 August, the troops finally arrived, ill and exhausted, at an open field where they were required to do battle with a river at their backs and the sun in their eyes. The Portuguese forces lined up in square formation, and the troops of Abd al-Malik in a crescent. The Moroccan forces, composed of well-trained light cavalry and harquebusiers, were able to manoeuvre with great agility.

An eye-witness recorded that at one point during the day a 'dark hour' arrived when the heat was so great, the din, the smoke, the dust, and the shouting were so overwhelming, and the confusion so complete, that it was scarcely possible to see how the defeat came about. The same witness also affirmed that no one who claimed to be able to relate what had occurred was credible, as it was impossible to see anything. It all happened in a blinding flash, a demonstration of 'the wrath of God who blinded them all'.

Don Sebastian died in combat. The Jewish doctor to sultan Abd al-Malik later certified that the Portuguese king died as a consequence of two wounds, one to the head and another to an arm. The same doctor added that Don Sebastian's body was in Alcazar, in a box filled with lime. The Portuguese found it impossible to admit to the death of their king for some time: rumours abounded that the corpse had been disfigured, or that it was unidentified or falsely identified so as to give Don Sebastian time to escape. In time, a myth formed according to which the man who had been the central cause of the whole catastrophe and of Portugal's tragic loss became, in the eyes of his compatriots, the Saviour of Future Times: a truly messianic emperor, the 'hidden' one who wandered the world purging his sins, and those of his people, before returning in triumph at the End of all Time to lead Portugal, the chosen nation, on to its ultimate and triumphant destiny. Such ideas led to the development of a current of thought – 'Sebastianism' – that provides evidence for how widespread messianic, eschatological thought and providentialist feeling were throughout both the Christian and Islamic Mediterranean in the sixteenth century. This brand of thinking will recur further along in our story.

Don Sebastian's advisers knew the importance of his opponent, Abd al-Malik, who had made himself known in Europe through skilful diplomatic activity. But the dimensions of the disaster resounded

all over Europe and definitively altered the way Morocco was perceived, especially by those Northern European countries that
struggled against Iberian hegemony. They suddenly found a possible
new ally.

Muley Abd al-Malik al-Sa'di

If Don Sebastian was right about anything, it was that the Moroccans
were afraid of him. In Morocco the memory of the loss of the cities of
Ceuta and Tangier was still fresh, and they had tried in vain to recover
them. The loss of Ceuta, in particular, conquered by the Portuguese
in 1415, had had a devastating impact. Not only was Ceuta an important city, but this was the first time that Moroccans – until then accustomed to crossing the Strait of Gibraltar on missions of conquest or
intervention in Peninsular affairs – had seen events turn against
them.

The memory of the loss of Granada was also still alive, and it had
driven a large number of exiles, known as *andalusiyyun* or
'Andalusians' (those who came from al-Andalus), to Morocco. Even
more vivid was the memory of the recent War of the Alpujarras in
the mountainous regions of Granada, fought between the Spanish
crown and Muslims forced to convert to Christianity, the 'Moriscos'.
That war had ended in another terrible defeat for the Muslims and a
second wave of emigration to Morocco.

Arabic sources record the panic and anxiety of the Moroccan
population as King Sebastian approached the country with his army.
The city of Fez, for example, was virtually empty of its inhabitants,
who had fled to the remotest regions of the nearby Atlas Mountains.
Abd al-Malik hastily ordered new fortifications for his capital
Marrakesh, gathering all manner of masons, builders, carpenters and
smiths for the task, whether 'Muslim or Christian', in the words of
the sources. Above all, Abd al-Malik set about organizing and supplying his army with great efficiency, and, with the aid of his brother
Ahmad, placed several contingents around those areas where it
was thought the Portuguese were most likely to disembark. The

Moroccans did not know until 1 August that the Portuguese would disembark at Asila. After Don Sebastian's departure from Tangier, they were expecting him to disembark at Larache, and that is why the two brothers and their troops were encamped just outside Rabat, a short journey from the site where the Portuguese army was expected to land.

While they were waiting there, Abd al-Malik ate a little fish and melon and drank a large amount of water. Something disagreed with him, and he began to vomit and suffer from the effects of a high fever. A detailed report on the sultan's illness and the measures taken to remedy it has survived intact. It is written in the form of a lengthy letter in Spanish; though anonymous, it appears to have been written by the sultan's Jewish doctor to his brother. The letter is kept in the Public Record Office in London together with a contemporary English translation, suggesting the interest the battle aroused throughout Europe, and the difficulty of finding reliable information about it.

Abd al-Malik's doctor describes the course of the sultan's illness in great detail, and the measures he took to try to cure it. He writes that he went out in a state of alarm to Abd al-Malik's brother, Muley Ahmad, to tell him about it, and was ordered to keep the illness a secret. He describes a brief improvement in the sultan's condition, during which, on the eve of the battle, Abd al-Malik asked to be dressed in brocade, with plumes, precious stones and a turban. Abd al-Malik girded himself with the sword he had brought with him from Turkey and his dagger, both of which were richly adorned with turquoise stones and rubies. Finally he placed all of his largest, most valuable rings on his fingers and, disobeying the doctor's orders, rode out to view his troops. Both kings, Don Sebastian and Abd al-Malik, appeared on the battlefield in their most luxurious clothing.

The first clash led to the breaking of the Moroccan front line, the line of 'our people', in the words of the anonymous Jewish doctor. Abd al-Malik swiftly reorganized his troops with great verve and fury, gave an order to attack and then suddenly fainted and fell from his horse. The doctor went to him quickly, pretended to give him water to drink and helped him on to his litter, where he died instantly. The anonymous doctor then went straight to Muley Ahmad – 'may God extol him', he writes – to break the news secretly, and the sultan's brother assumed immediate command of the troops. Meanwhile the doctor himself spent the rest of the battle running back and forth between Muley Ahmad and the litter where the sultan's body lay, pretending to transmit Abd al-Malik's orders to his brother so as to prevent alarm among the Moroccan troops. He continued to do this until the end of the battle, when 'miraculously God took the kingdom of Portugal and delivered it over to these peoples'.

The doctor was most likely Joseph Valencia, who was later personal physician to Abd al-Malik's brother, Ahmad al-Mansur. Valencia is described in Portuguese accounts as a man of great presence and 'gentrified in the Spanish manner'. He was an expert in Arabic medicine who read Avicenna in Hebrew translation. Of the Greek and Latin schools of medicine, he knew only Galen, in Arabic translation. Despite his limitations, Portuguese captives later wrote, Valencia's long experience was respected by Portuguese doctors. In his letter to his brother, Valencia catalogued the immediate consequences of the battle of Alcazar as follows:

> This kingdom became so rich in gold and silver and weapons of every kind, and mules, horses and oxen, that there is now no gunner left who wishes to serve, nor any Negro who did not become as wealthy as his lords. I cannot, sir, express to you how much it was and he who did not see it would not believe it.

According to Valencia, there were so many captives that even the humblest of Moroccans had a Christian page in his service, and Muslim labourers no longer felt compelled to earn a living because all had two or three captives working for them. The new sultan Muley Ahmad kept all the captured Portuguese noblemen for himself. One such captive *hidalgo*, Antonio de Saldanha (who later wrote an account of his life in Morocco), recorded that Muley Ahmad ordered all Portuguese boys under the age of fifteen who had taken part in the battle to be sought out and converted to Islam. They were circumcised and made to wear Moroccan dress. The sultan, Saldanha continues, left three hundred of these boys in Fez and took the rest of them with him to Marrakesh to serve in his palace as personal pages. Muley Ahmad, henceforth known as al-Mansur, 'The Victorious', entered Fez with his army a few days after the battle. He brought with him a huge number of captives, all the equipment of the defeated Portuguese army, and the corpse of his dead brother. Muley Abd al-Malik was buried with great ceremony in Fez on 16 August.

From this point on, Arabic chronicles and European records provide evidence of interest in the new sultan, Muley Ahmad. Arabic authors set about aggrandizing the new monarch by telling prodigious anecdotes about him as a child, with a destiny foretold, as well as stories of his vigorous personality evinced by the two new marriages he made immediately after the battle. According to some of these sources, Muley Ahmad's importance had been singled out by his very own ancestor, the Prophet Muhammad. European chroniclers sought to understand the new monarch's tastes, characteristics and political ambitions, but what really had happened during the first thirty years of Ahmad's life? And what sort of country did he rule when he came to the throne?

2

ABD AL-MALIK AND AHMAD
BEFORE THE BATTLE OF
ALCAZAR

Most of what can be understood about Muley Ahmad al-Mansur's life before his accession to the throne must be deduced from what is known of the life of his brother, Abd al-Malik, with whom he shared almost twenty years of exile. Abd al-Malik was a brilliant man who attracted a great deal of attention among his contemporaries, and ample documentation concerning him has survived. He laid the foundations for the administrative reforms and improvements in diplomatic relations that would be continued by his brother Ahmad. Above all, Abd al-Malik undertook a complete restructuring of the armed forces with regard to instruction, organization and recruitment. Brief though it was, Abd al-Malik's reign undoubtedly shaped the nation that his brother inherited.

Abd al-Malik, the second son of Muhammad al-Shaykh (the first sultan of the Sa'dian dynasty), was born in 1541. When his brother Abdallah assumed the throne in 1557, he fled first to Tlemcen and then to Algiers and Istanbul, together with his brothers Abd al-Mu'min and Ahmad. Ahmad, born in 1549, was eight years younger than Abd al-Malik. It is not clear that Ahmad always accompanied his older brother, but we do know that Abd al-Mu'min stayed in Tlemcen, where he was given a post by the Turks and where, years later, he was assassinated by henchmen sent by his brother Abdallah. The fact that Abd al-Mu'min was the only brother disposed of in this way may indicate that he was the only one in Tlemcen at this moment. However, it is clear that Ahmad spent a considerable number of years in Tlemcen. In fact, although little is known about Muley Ahmad's first marriage, his eldest and favourite son, Muley Muhammad al-Shaykh al-Ma'mun, was born in Tlemcen and was educated at the city's *madrasa*, a centre of learning renowned throughout the Islamic West. Ahmad, as we will see, was a man of profound Islamic learning, a lover of books, calligraphy and mathematics, as well as a connoisseur of mystical texts and a lover of scholarly discussions. Such traditional Arabo-Islamic knowledge was probably acquired, at least in part, in the city of Fez before Ahmad's exile at the age of seventeen, but there is no question that it would have been easier for him to continue such studies in Tlemcen, a city of scholars, rather than in Algiers, a city of traders, military men and corsairs. The names of several of his masters in Tlemcen are known. His love of the Eastern form of Arabic calligraphy may also have been acquired in Istanbul or in Cairo, cities that his brother Abd al-Malik is known to have visited. Once in power, Muley Ahmad established the first academic chair in calligraphy in Morocco.

Ahmad and Abd al-Malik were only half-brothers. They had different mothers, and it is Abd al-Malik's mother who is known to have spent some time in Istanbul. Ahmad does not seem to have known or admired the Turks as much as his brother did, or to have spoken Turkish as well as Abd al-Malik. But Ahmad's military knowledge can hardly have been acquired by any other means than enrolment in the Ottoman army – in this, he must have followed Abd al-Malik. What is clear is that the brothers were closely united when they returned to Morocco, where they showed an intimacy and trust that was probably forged during their long exile together. The extent of this trust can be gauged from the fact that Ahmad made several secret journeys to Morocco disguised as a merchant to make contact with leading men and tribal chieftains loyal to Abd al-Malik, and to recruit followers there. Arabic sources hint that Ahmad was the emissary and the 'eyes' of Abd al-Malik in Morocco, providing him with first-hand information on the current situation there. During these secret missions, Ahmad would carry precious stones with him, especially

Burmese rubies, to make his identity as a merchant more credible and to smooth the path with wavering followers. Ahmad's knowledge and appreciation of precious stones became legendary among those who knew him.

In conclusion, there is no firm evidence that Ahmad stayed in Tlemcen throughout his exile but he certainly spent most of it there; nor is there evidence that he was with Abd al-Malik in the years his brother spent in Algiers and Istanbul, though he appears to have visited these major urban centres. What we do know for certain is that Ahmad's brother Abd al-Malik spent most of his exile in the city of Algiers.

ALGIERS

Half a century earlier, Algiers had been conquered by Aruj and Khayr al-Din Barbarossa, brothers and pirates of Greek origin, with military aid from Istanbul. Under the Barbarossas, the so-called Regency of Algiers became the main centre of Ottoman authority in the Maghreb, and the base from which the Ottomans were able to wage war on Spain, including its provinces in southern Italy. Above all, it was the main base from which Muslim corsairs set out on their missions of undeclared war on the marginal areas of the northern Mediterranean. These corsair ships were chartered, provisioned and armed by private individuals to whom the authorities in Algiers (and other Mediterranean ports) granted letters of marque (letters that certified their condition as privateers) to attack Christian ships and coasts. The booty derived from such missions usually took the form of men who were taken as captives to Algiers, a city whose income was mainly derived from the payments of ransom money for such prisoners. The *beylerbey* or governor of Algiers exercised sovereignty, in the name of the Ottoman sultan, over the *pashas* of Tripoli and Tunis, and thereby constituted the greatest Ottoman authority in the Western Mediterranean. In North Africa, only Morocco lay outside the orbit of Turkish control.

Under the Turks, Algiers became a crowded, cosmopolitan and wealthy city in a state of permanent turmoil. It was large, with a population equal to or greater than that of Palermo or Rome. Located in a precipitous bay protected by a number of small islets that made it almost impregnable, it was fortified by the Barbarossas and had a well-planned centre built up with wealthy private mansions. Algiers was a port city with great trading activity and an extremely varied population, and European travellers who visited it in the mid-sixteenth century described it as prosperous, pleasant and beautiful, full of magnificent houses, public baths, formidable fortifications and sumptuous religious buildings. Fortunes were rapidly made and there were plenty of opportunities for social mobility. Berbers, Turks and Arabs, as well as Spanish Muslims or Andalusians, Jews, captives and Renegades from all parts of Europe resided there. In the streets of Algiers it was possible to hear all of the languages of the Mediterranean.

Of all the population of Algiers, the Renegades probably constituted the largest group: they comprised the former inhabitants of the poorest regions of southern Europe, Sicilians, Sardinians, Calabrians, Greeks and Corsicans, some of whom had arrived of their own free will but most as captives. Simple conversion to Islam was enough to allow such men to integrate into the corsair society of Algiers, nothing else being required beyond their own ability or adventurous spirit. Contemporary European literature dwells on the most daring endeavours, triumphant returns and rich banquets of the corsairs, and on their lives of luxury and wastefulness: the 'Indies and Peru' of the Mediterranean, as it was called ironically by Miguel de Cervantes, the author of *Don Quixote* and the best-known of all the Algiers captives.

In Algiers, Abd al-Malik married the daughter of a Turkish high dignitary, Hajji Murat, and they had a son, Muley Isma'il. Abd al-Malik maintained close ties with a series of governors of Algiers, and constantly negotiated for Turkish support for his return to Morocco to regain the throne.

ABD AL-MALIK'S PROPAGANDA

In Algiers, Abd al-Malik was a well-known and distinguished figure.
He appears to have been held in high popular esteem; Cervantes,
who was captive in the city during the period when Abd al-Malik was
still living there, portrayed him in one of his comedies: 'He knows the
Turkish language, the Spanish and the German, the Italian and the
French. He sleeps in a bed and eats at a table, sitting at it in the manner of the Christians. Above all he is a great soldier, generous, wise,
self-possessed, endowed with a thousand virtues.'

Cervantes noted Abd al-Malik's 'Christian' customs – his habit of
eating at a table and sleeping in a bed – as signs that he had adopted
European decorum. Thus, according to Cervantes, Abd al-Malik was
a highly civilized man, who appreciated Christian manners and may
have even aspired to Christian 'virtues'. Abd al-Malik's Muslim contemporaries generally used little furniture. They ate seated on large
pillows placed on carpets and woven mats on the ground about round
tables comprising large trays on low stands, and they slept on mats
and long baskets that were unfurled on the floor at night. Cervantes
clearly felt some sympathy towards Abd al-Malik and may have
wished to convey those feelings to his Spanish public, who would
have understood from this description that Abd al-Malik had philo-
Christian leanings – that he was a 'noble' Moor. Religious affiliation
was identified in the sixteenth-century Mediterranean world by
manners and protocols of dress, dining and comportment.
Cervantes' description may or may not be based on direct observa-
tion, but it absolutely conforms with the image of himself that
Abd al-Malik wanted to transmit to the northern shore of the
Mediterranean.

Comfortable in several cultures and capable of speaking many
languages, that Abd al-Malik was careful to polish his image for the
benefit of Europeans can be perceived in his relationship with his contemporaries Elizabeth I of England, Henri III of France and Philip II.
Edmund Hogan, the English ambassador who visited Abd al-Malik in
1577, compared him to Protestants in letters to the Queen: 'finding

him to be a verie earnest Protestant of good religion and well experimented as well in the Old Testament as the New'. Interestingly, different qualities were expressed in a Spanish Dominican's panegyric published in Valencia in 1576 and directed to the Spanish nation. Recalling Cervantes' admiration, the Dominican friar praised the sultan by emphasizing his European characteristics and implied that there were pro-Catholic and pro-Spanish elements in his character. 1576 was the year when Abd al-Malik ascended the throne, and the panegyric contained within it the seeds of hope for an alliance.

The panegyric was published by Francisco Gasparo Corso, a member of a sort of office of propaganda and public relations run by Abd al-Malik. The Gasparo Corso brothers were important corsair merchants who managed an agency devoted to diplomatic and trading activities between the northern Mediterranean states and Muslim countries. The agency specialized in translating reports for several courts and negotiating commercial transactions between Europe and the Islamic world. Francisco lived in Valencia, while Andrea, the most famous of the brothers, ran the office in Algiers, where he became a close adviser to Abd al-Malik. When Abd al-Malik came to the throne in 1576, Andrea followed him to Marrakesh and was appointed an agent of the sultan in charge of relations with the Spanish and Portuguese governments. The other three Gasparo Corso brothers settled in Algiers, Marseille and Barcelona, points from which they ran their growing commercial agency. The work of the Gasparo Corso brothers, like that of other contemporaries, illustrates the range of mechanisms available for the handling of diplomatic and commercial relations between the Islamic and European worlds, despite the levels of hostility in the Mediterranean. There were various institutions that operated on the margins of and across the seemingly impermeable barrier.

There is some evidence that Abd al-Malik spoke Spanish well, as did his brother Abd al-Mu'min. Both had been brought up at a court where there were many courtiers of Spanish origin, as well as a large number of Spaniards among the sultan's slaves and concubines.

Abd al-Malik may well have learnt Italian in Algiers, either through his friendship with the Gasparo Corso brothers or through Turkish dignitaries. For example, the mother tongue of the Turkish governor of Algiers, Hassan Pasha, was Tuscan. A Spanish friar by the name of Fray Luis Nieto, an eye-witness of the battle of Alcazar who wrote an account of it that was translated into several languages, described Abd al-Malik as follows: 'he spoke our Spanish tongue very clearly and knew how to write it; he had a high level in the Italian tongue, and he spoke the Turkish tongue better than any other except his natural [first] language which was Arabic, in which he was a singular poet'. His description is consistent with Cervantes' high praise.

Abd al-Malik was clearly a man of talent with a surprisingly modern grasp of the uses of propaganda. The campaign to reinforce his image as a man inclined to European, Christian mores was accompanied by the establishment of diplomatic contact with Philip II of Spain. Abd al-Malik tried to negotiate mutual projects of alliance including a proposal to conquer Algiers together, in exchange, naturally, for Spanish assistance in regaining the Moroccan throne. Philip II did not respond to these propositions, but was happy to receive the reports on Turkish affairs and the Regency of Algiers that were sent to him regularly by Abd al-Malik through the Gasparo Corso agency. Philip's contact with Abd al-Malik – which continued after Abd al-Malik regained power in Morocco – and his high opinion of him were compelling reasons, however, to refuse to support Don Sebastian's expedition to Africa.

Meanwhile, Abd al-Malik enrolled in the Ottoman army, where he became an excellent military leader. He seems to have completed his army training in Istanbul, where he moved with part of his family (or, at the very least, with his mother). We know that he petitioned the Ottoman sultan, Selim II (r. 1566–74), for aid. But the long months of negotiation came to nothing, and Abd al-Malik felt forced to turn to Spain for assistance. As noted above, we do not know whether his brother Ahmad accompanied him during his stay in the Ottoman capital.

Abd al-Malik fought on the Ottoman side in 1571 in the great sea battle of Lepanto. This battle, pitched between the Ottomans and the huge armada of the Holy League comprising the Papacy, the Republic of Venice and the Spanish crown, ended in a crushing defeat for the Ottomans. The Ottoman navy was destroyed, and although it was able to recover slightly in the years that followed, the Turkish role in the Mediterranean was permanently reduced by the predominance of the Spanish navy. Lepanto was a terrible psychological blow for the whole of the Muslim Mediterranean, and for this reason the Ottoman conquest of Spanish-controlled Tunis in 1574 assumed great symbolic significance. Abd al-Malik played a leading role in the Ottoman reconquest of Tunis, and later made much use of that role in the propaganda he directed at both his Moroccan subjects and his Ottoman patrons, to whom he was able to present himself as a champion of the *jihad*. In fact, it was Abd al-Malik's brilliant participation in the conquest of Tunis and the nearby fortress of La Goleta which led the new Ottoman caliph, Murat III (1574–95), to support his candidacy to the throne of Morocco.

Arabic sources relate, in a manner combining hagiography and legend, that Abd al-Malik's mother, the widowed sultana Sahaba al-Rahmaniyya, then living in Istanbul, heard of the success of the Tunis mission through her son's envoys before the news reached the court at the Topkapi Palace. She hurried to tell the Caliph Murat about it, asking as a reward that the caliph would give assistance to Abd al-Malik in his quest to gain the Moroccan throne. Murat agreed, and Abd al-Malik and his mother travelled to Algiers with a document that instructed the governor of the city to supply him with all the troops he needed. Shortly afterwards, in December 1575, Abd al-Malik and his brother Ahmad left Algiers with two thousand Janissaries (Ottoman soldiers of slave origin). His wife and son stayed behind in Algiers on the insistence of the Turks and as a guarantee that Abd al-Malik, after regaining his throne, would abide by the conditions stipulated by his patrons, which included suzerainty of the Ottomans over Morocco. In fact, things did not work out quite this way and Abd al-Malik sent the Janissaries back to Algiers as soon as he had defeated his nephew.

When Abd al-Malik returned to Morocco, he had lived in Ottoman lands for twenty-eight years (from the age of sixteen to thirty-four). He dressed in the Turkish style, spoke Turkish and felt great admiration for Ottoman institutions, especially the army. Moreover, as was common among many of his Turkish contemporaries, he was highly curious about European modes and fashions and spoke several European languages. Abd al-Malik was greatly influenced by constant contact with captives and Renegades from many European countries. Edmund Hogan, the English ambassador to Morocco, described with interest Abd al-Malik's urbane customs, such as his enthusiasm for European music, and the musicians he had brought to him from England. He also mentions Abd al-Malik's interest in sporting activities hitherto unknown in Morocco, such as hunting ducks with water-spaniels or baiting bulls with dogs. In the gardens of his palace in Agedal, he had a large rectangular pond, with a ship he liked to sail in it. Hogan recorded how he was received by Abd al-Malik, who was surrounded by his Christian and Muslim advisers: 'And his councellors being as well Moores as Christians, standing about him, I dutifullie delyverid your Majesties letters and declared my message in Spanische.' This message was duly accepted by Abd al-Malik, who 'answered me againe in Spanishe'. Abd al-Malik not only spoke and wrote good Spanish but was also in the habit of signing the diplomatic letters that his officials sent to European courts in Latin script, using the form 'Abdelmeleq'. We know from other sources how delighted he always was to receive his friend Andrea Gasparo Corso in Morocco, who would bring him anchovies, cheese and other favourite delicacies that could not be found locally.

The court historian al-Ifrani recorded that 'he was a man inclined towards novelties'. The word 'novelties' has connotations of heterodoxy, or at least reprehensible innovation in Islamic law. In fact, as soon as he came to the throne Abd al-Malik initiated wide-ranging reforms of the Moroccan administration and its system of tax collection. The object of most of his reforming zeal was the army, which was reorganized along Turkish lines, even to the extent of applying Turkish terms to the ranking of officers.

Although Abd al-Malik hoped to maintain Morocco outside the orbit of Turkish sovereignty, the great admiration he felt for the

Ottoman world is conspicuous. He was so persuaded that the Ottoman model was the right one for Morocco that he asked Edmund Hogan to instruct English merchants to export large quantities of cloth to Morocco; he had decided to change his subjects' clothing and to oblige them all to dress in the Turkish fashion. But he did not have time to bring about this ambitious reform. He reigned for only two years, and when his brother Ahmad succeeded him he did not show the same enthusiasm for Turkish models and fashions. What Ahmad did learn from his brother, however, was how to carve out a role for Morocco between the two great powers that threatened the country, the Ottomans and the Spanish. This was done by making offers, alliances and counter-alliances, playing one side off against the other and making the same sorts of promises to both. The intrinsic weakness of Morocco's position was to be used to great advantage.

From his arrival in Morocco until his death, Abd al-Malik was consistent in his presentation of his brother Ahmad as his heir. Ahmad played an important military role during the period of his brother's attempt to seize power, and also served him during his two years of government, first as his prime minister and next as governor of the city of Fez. Ahmad was officially confirmed as heir to the throne in a letter publicly addressed to him which read: 'Be it known to you that I do not love anyone, other than myself, the way I love you. And my desire is to hand over this matter [royal power] to you and to no one but you.' In this way Abd al-Malik deliberately showed great fondness, warmth and closeness towards his brother, who was then away on a military mission to suppress rebellions in the south of the country. Also, as it happens, he asked Ahmad to join him in fighting the invading forces of Don Sebastian.

MULEY AHMAD AL-MANSUR

Precisely because of his brother's brilliance, few people believed at the start of his reign that Muley Ahmad would be able to retain power for long. Indeed, only two months after the battle of Alcazar, Ahmad was faced with the first major challenge to his authority when his Andalusian troops rebelled against him and tried to lead what was effectively a coup d'état.

European nations soon started to send informers and embassies to Morocco, and more than one expressed doubts about the new sultan's chances of success. A Spanish report from the period stated wryly: 'We might well say that the said emperor finds himself at present in travail like a ship that is close to land, beaten back by two seas, without a wind, which neither lets him go forward nor back,' warning, 'And he will strike against land if God does not remedy his state with some wind to free him from danger.' The two 'seas' that the fragile Moroccan ship of state had to navigate were those of the Turks and the Spanish. But all European nations, Catholic and Protestant alike, sought to establish good relations with Morocco.

From Moroccan chronicles, we learn that when Ahmad came to the throne, he was a man of about thirty years of age, tall and well-built, with rounded cheeks, a golden-brown complexion, black hair and eyes, and remarkably white teeth. He was married and had children. Of a kindly disposition and elegant manners, Ahmad was a shy man who lost his temper easily and whose anger was fearsome. He had a great liking for luxury and a taste for extravagance. He was very generous, as only one can be, the Arab chronicler tells us, who knows no fear of the future. He was the son of Mesuda, the daughter of a famous southern *shaykh* from the region of Ouarzazate, said to have been a highly educated and pious woman. Greatly interested in architecture and building, Mesuda financed and supervised the construction of several religious and civic buildings in Marrakesh, some of which survive today. The sources inform us that she educated her son Ahmad, who was very close to her, in wisdom and virtue, and from the moment she placed his first amulets on him he displayed all the signs of royal authority. They also inform us that he was the youngest and favourite son of his father, Muley Muhammad al-Shaykh, who, like a character in a popular tale, had foreseen that his youngest son would one day inherit the great destinies that he, the founder of the dynasty, had laid out for him and for which (again according to the stuff of legend) he was envied by his older brother Abdallah.

More prosaically, European observers tended to emphasize Ahmad's love of hunting. The new sultan organized lion-shoots in the region of Marrakesh and enjoyed hunting birds with falcons. He also used eagles to hunt gazelles, and one foreign agent recorded how spectacular it was to see these eagles grasp and hold on to a gazelle until one of the hunters on foot or horseback arrived to cut its throat. All varieties of birds, the same authority recorded, were hunted with falcons, including large ones such as buzzards which would sometimes jump straight into the hands of the hunters for fear of the falcons.

Ahmad also had a love of horses and always kept several excellent animals for riding. When he was travelling, his letters to secretaries and governors often included instructions for the care of his horses and concern for their well-being. When the British trading company known as the Barbary Company was established in Morocco, one of the first actions of its founders, Augustine and Ralph Lane, was to send a Moroccan falcon to England as an object of curiosity. They also bought up a number of thoroughbred horses, but Muley Ahmad refused permission for the animals to be exported, alluding to the Qur'anic precept (Q. 46:5) that considers horses noble beasts necessary for the waging of holy war, so that it was against doctrine to sell them to non-Muslims. Ahmad al-Mansur was also an excellent military leader, who had spent a great deal of time fighting throughout his country and had a profound understanding of his troops and the way an army should function. His chroniclers invariably report that he was very brave.

However, all observers agreed that if the new sultan had one interest over and above his love of hunting and horses, it was his enthusiasm for precious stones. In Spain this penchant was well-known as, even before ascending the throne, Ahmad had bought stones through the Duke of Medinasidonia. Throughout his reign, Ahmad sent trustworthy servants, mainly Jews, all over Europe in search of particular items. In 1579, he received an ambassador from Philip II, Pedro

Venegas de Córdoba, who brought with him a series of gifts of such splendour that the sultan's attention was completely absorbed. They included a ruby said to be as large as the palm of a hand (most likely a balas ruby from Afghanistan), an emerald the size of an apple that blinded all who saw it (probably from Colombia), a necklace with twelve rubies, and 120 ounces of pearls, some of them the size of walnuts. All of these jewels were procured by Spain via the Indian Ocean trade, with the exception of the emeralds. These jewels were mainly bought by the Mughals and Spain had a lively trade with them in Colombian emeralds. The largest ones were almost always saved to send to India, and in this sense it is more extraordinary that such an emerald was given to Ahmad as a diplomatic gift. Philip's extravagant gifts, sent as a token of friendship, caused the sultan to treat the Spanish ambassador with the greatest of kindness, whereas he was very cold, at least in the presence of the Spanish representative, towards the Portuguese ambassador Francisco da Costa, and the Englishman Edmund Hogan. His own ambassador to England, Sidi al-Hajj Massa, fell into disgrace when it was proved that he had brought back to Morocco two large rubies, purchased while abroad, that he had concealed from his sovereign.

Muley Ahmad never spoke to any stranger except through an interpreter; he did so as a show of hieraticism and majesty, but also because he spoke very little other than Arabic. Ahmad was not as Turkified as his brother, though he shared Abd al-Malik's curiosity for all things European. We know, for example, that he asked for detailed progress reports on the building of Philip II's palace of El Escorial, and followed the construction process as closely as he could from abroad. Also, like contemporary European monarchs and their Ottoman counterparts, he decided to have his portrait painted, asking Philip II in January 1592 to send him a portrait painter. This task was assigned, like all other Moroccan business, to the Duke of Medinasidonia, who sent a painter by the name of Blas de Prado. Prado (1545–99) was a painter of some distinction, master of Sánchez Cotán, both of them creators of a famous style of still-lifes. The artist stayed at the Moroccan court until 1598, when he returned to Madrid with a letter from Muley Ahmad expressing the sultan's satisfaction with Prado's portrait of him. Unfortunately, the painting has not survived.

What has survived, however, is a portrait of the Moroccan ambassador at the English court, Sidi Abd al-Wahid Annuri, in a curious Tudor style, now in the collection of Birmingham University in England (see Chapter 5). It is widely believed that Islam forbids the representation of animate beings and it is true that many Islamic societies, especially those of the Arab Middle East, have a traditional distrust of representations of human beings. However, in other Islamic cultures, such as the Turkish, Persian and Indian, portraiture played an important role in the construction of the imperial image. In the fifteenth century, the Ottoman sultan Mehmet II, who had close ties with the Venetian Republic, requested that the artist Giovanni Bellini be sent to Istanbul to paint his portrait (now in the National Gallery in London); and after him almost all Ottoman sultans had their portraits painted. When Ahmad commissioned a portrait, he was probably emulating the Ottoman practice.

Muley Ahmad was a 'modern' monarch with an interest in novelties, from whatever source. In both European and Moroccan chronicles, he emerges as a man with an interest in knowledge, intellectually curious and with a well-trained memory. He received an extensive education in Islamic religious and secular sciences, including theology, law, poetry, grammar, lexicography, exegesis, geometry, arithmetics and algebra, and astronomy. One of his professors wrote a catalogue (in Arabic, a *fihrist*) of the subjects Ahmad had studied, the books he had read and discussed and the scholars who had been his teachers; those with the highest reputations taught him in Fez and in Tlemcen, where he obviously spent a large part of his exile.

Arabic sources provide details of his passionate love of study, and describe him as 'the caliph of the wise and the wise man of the caliphs'. He was careful to organize his work in such a way that he had time for daily discussion and reading with scholars in the palace mosque. These sessions were given over to analysis of texts of the

Qur'an and Sayings of the Prophet, but also to rhetoric, logic, calculus and geometry. The sultan had specialists brought to him from all over the country and abroad to take part in these sessions. His greatest interest was in mathematics: his court historian al-Ifrani relates that he acquired an Arabic translation of Euclid, and as there was no-one at court who knew much geometry, he worked through theorem after theorem by himself.

He was also very keen on astrology and all of the sciences related to the stars, which included the interpretation of conjunctions and prediction of future events. In 1600, on the occasion of the arrival in England of the Moroccan ambassador Sidi Abd el-Wahid, the English merchant Thomas Bernhere wrote to his brother-in-law, the mathematician Edward Wright, to relate Muley Ahmad's love of astronomy and astrology and his wish to purchase 'instruments serving for the course of the sun and moon' and 'the motions of the heavens'. Muley Ahmad was especially interested in magnetic compasses and mathematical experiments on the lodestone. He also ordered his ambassador to acquire quadrants, astrolabes and maps of new regions. Bernhere sent instructions showing how the instruments were to be fabricated in brass or silver, leaving room for the Arabic words and numbers to be engraved on them, accompanied by a design of the instrument on paper in which the words to be engraved were written in Spanish. Sidi Abd el-Wahid may well have been portrayed in a similar way to Holbein's rendering of the French ambassadors of 1533, the enigmatic painting of the two men before a table full of astronomical instruments, now in the National Gallery in London.

Ahmad al-Mansur also corresponded with Muslim scholars in the Middle East. For the sake of this correspondence, and because of his love of calligraphy, he learned to write in Eastern scripts (quite different from the archaicized North African scripts), at which he excelled. He wrote several letters to Abu l-Hassan al-Bakri in Cairo that contained pictograms, one representing a garden, another representing two eyes.

Ahmad al-Mansur was a meticulous man. He surrounded himself with a group of secretaries who were required to be at court permanently, always on call. These secretaries, the most famous of whom was al-Fishtali, wrote beautifully calligraphed letters in convoluted rhymed prose, salted with Qur'anic quotations, Prophetic traditions, and poems, and ornamented with coloured inks. Ahmad was very keen to supervise the work of his secretaries, checking that adequate protocol was observed according to the rank of the recipient, often adding notes in his own hand. He also devised a cipher or encoded writing for secret letters. He spent a lot of time with his secretarial corps. On one occasion, he saw that al-Fishtali was fretting, and asked about the cause. He was told that al-Fishtali's child was ill. Al-Mansur declared that the best treatment for sick children was 'the remedies of old women' and that there were some excellent ones in his household. He had al-Fishtali's child brought to the palace (where, by the way, there was also an excellent physician). This incident was recorded as something extraordinary in the Arabic chronicles and as evidence that al-Mansur paid attention to little things and was full of affection for the people who surrounded him.

He was a great book collector and amassed a magnificent library of manuscripts. The printing press was not used in the Arabo-Islamic world, where it was considered less trustworthy than copying by hand; for example, misprints could corrupt the meaning and interpretation of Qur'anic verses. He sent messengers to several Islamic cities to purchase books for him and ordered some of his favourite works – such as compendiums of works by mystics – to be copied, illuminated, richly bound and embossed in gold. Many of them have marginal notes written in his own hand. He employed a number of scribes at court, including Moroccans, Andalusians and Middle Eastern scholars, and he liked to supervise their work personally. Books on Sufism or written by Sufi masters were among his favourites.

Ahmad's magnificent library grew to be one of his most precious possessions, and was inherited upon his death by his son Muley Zidan. In 1616, when Zidan was forced to leave the city of Marrakesh (at that time under siege by a rebel commander of armed forces opposed to the dynasty), he decided to take his personal belongings out of the city and put them on a ship in the port of Safi for safe transport to the north of the country, which remained loyal to him. Unfortunately for Zidan, the ship he chose for this delicate mission was a French privateer, which was pursued at sea by Spanish ships. The Spanish ships intercepted and captured the vessel, and, as a result, most of Muley Ahmad's magnificent library is now in the Biblioteca Real of the palace of El Escorial outside Madrid, and today constitutes one of the most significant collections of Arabic manuscripts in Europe.

Very little is known about Ahmad's family life. In 1579, soon after he inherited the throne, Ahmad named his eldest son, Muhammad al-Shaykh al-Ma'mun, as his successor and appointed him governor of Fez. He seems to have loved Muhammad deeply. Muhammad al-Shaykh's mother was Khayzuran, a black concubine, who was also beloved by the sultan and was mother to another of his sons, Abu Faris. He named a pavilion at the palace of al-Badi' after her. Later, he appointed three other sons to governorships of different regions of the country. The Arabic chronicles mention the mothers of these sons, who accompanied them to the cities where they were appointed. There are also letters from al-Mansur in which he names two of his daughters with terms of endearment. The letters preserved in chronicles that al-Mansur wrote to his sons are full of affection and care, advising the young governors on diverse matters of state as well as on simple, everyday matters. Al-Mansur was close to his own mother, Mesuda. Like her, Muley Ahmad was fascinated by architecture and the construction of beautiful buildings, many of which survive in his capital, Marrakesh. There is no record in the sources of debauchery, affairs with slaves or cruelty, though reports of such behaviour abound in the records of the lives of his sons. Indeed, three of his sons – Zidan, Abu Faris and Muhammad al-Shaykh – would quarrel over the throne after his death in 1603.

What we are able to know about Ahmad al-Mansur as a sovereign must be deduced from his political and diplomatic activity, the subject of the chapters that follow. Arabic sources insist on presenting a grand image of a cultured, pious ruler with a love of learning and of mystical thought: half saint and half warrior. Almost all the authors of such reports were official court chroniclers, whose work was written in the service of the sultan, and was financed and managed by him. They reflect an image of their sovereign which requires decoding. In order to proceed, we need to examine the country that Ahmad came to rule, and in particular the political forces and groupings that were current during his reign.

3

SIXTEENTH-CENTURY MOROCCO: ITS POPULATION, CITIES, RELIGIOUS ELITES AND ARMY

Like most pre-modern nations, sixteenth-century Morocco was a largely rural territory sparsely punctuated by cities. It was a spectacularly extensive land, very varied geographically, from Mediterranean and Atlantic coasts to desert, from high mountains to plains. Its limits coincide with the borders of the present-day Morocco: it included the wide Atlantic plains where cattle grazed and cereal was grown, the circle of the Atlas mountains from the Rif in the north abruptly bordering the Mediterranean coast, through the Middle to the High Atlas near Marrakesh. The High Atlas rises from the edge of the desert to Alpine scenery, reaching as high as 3700 metres (12,000 ft). The high pastures were summer grazing grounds for the flocks of the Saharan nomads coming from the southern slopes, as well as for the animals of the mountain tribesmen who lived in the more fertile valleys of the northern slopes. Those slopes gave way to the irrigable lands of the Sous river in the north and in the south to the Ziz and Dra'a valleys that mark the course of the trans-Saharan routes. Silver and copper mines were to be found in the Saharan valleys. It was a country divided by high mountains and communications were difficult. The western end of the Atlas range was reached and crossed from south to north by nomadic merchants. In the oases among the nomadic tribes of the Sahara, the Berbers had, from the 'Middle Ages' (here delimiting the period from the eighth to the fifteenth centuries), organized the desert trade to supply the markets of the Mediterranean with Negroes from the central Sudan and with gold from the banks of the Niger.

THE POPULATION OF MOROCCO: ARABS AND BERBERS

Morocco was an island surrounded by sea and desert with a low population density. The earliest population registers in Morocco did not become available until the twentieth century, during the period of French colonial rule, and even then there were only three million Moroccans in total. The figure can hardly have been higher in the late sixteenth century or during the seventeenth, given that the country was subject to regular and devastating epidemics of plague, such as the one that killed Ahmad al-Mansur. Famine was recurrent, and severe illnesses characteristic of sixteenth-century Europe, including the *morbo gallico* (syphilis), also found their way to Morocco.

Morocco was – and still is – inhabited by a mixed population of Arabs and Berbers. The Berbers constituted the native population of North Africa before the Arabo-Islamic conquest of the eighth century, an indigenous tribal population of peasants, transhumants and nomads. They had been partially romanized in the northern half of the region, in what was called Mauritania Tingitana. They were organized in tribes whose head was called *shaykh* in Arabic, *amghar* in Berber. The Berber tribes spoke a variety of Berber dialects. Though Islamicized and Arabized after the period of the conquest, most Berbers in Morocco continued to speak their own language, which coexisted with Arabic, as it does today. In the time of Ahmad al-Mansur, Berbers were largely Arabized in the plains and the cities. In the cities and coastal regions, Spanish and Portuguese were also spoken. Morocco was, as it is now, a multilingual society.

From the second half of the Middle Ages onward, that is, from the twelfth century, the dynasties of the Almohads and, to an even greater extent, their successors the Marinids resorted to the 'importation' into Morocco of Arab tribes from the Eastern and Central Maghreb. Nomadic Arab tribes were recruited for the armed forces and given lands in the Atlantic plains of Morocco which they used as sources of income through tax-farming. In addition to tax collection, these tribes worked in the ruling dynasties' armies. The importation of nomadic tribes contributed greatly to the Arabization of Morocco, but caused conflict with the Berber population; the Berbers, who were generally sedentary or transhumant and agricultural, took refuge from the Arab tribes in the mountainous regions of the Atlas, so as to protect themselves from raids and plunder. In addition, the Arab tribes often lived in the hinterland of the Atlantic ports controlled by the Portuguese and established alliances with them through trade, selling wheat to the Portuguese coastal strongholds. These Arab tribes were the groups described by Portuguese and Spanish sources as 'Moros de paz' or 'Treaty Moors'. Muley Ahmad, like his predecessors and successors, had frequent difficulties with these tribes, whose presence was a double-edged sword. One of the measures he adopted to guarantee their loyalty was to establish blood ties with them by promoting marriages between members of his dynasty and women of the tribes.

However, the distinction between Arabs and Berbers is not always clear. For example, the difference hardly existed in the cities. In Moroccan cities there was a long-standing Arab 'bourgeoisie' very distinct from the tribal Arabs of the Atlantic plains and the desert fringe. The prestige of an Arab lineage, like everything else linking the Islamic West and its peoples with the lands of the cradle of Islam, was so great that many Berber tribes had adopted such lineages long before, and had 'Arabized' themselves in language. This phenomenon is related to the fact that at the time of the Arab conquest of Morocco entire Berber tribes, upon converting to Islam, had associated themselves through *wala* or 'client' relationships with conquering Arab tribes whose names they adopted and whose members they married.

So, in some cases, there was no clear line of demarcation between Arabs and Berbers, and no state of permanent conflict between the two groups. Nonetheless, the distinction remained a factor in the countryside, making social cohesion more difficult, and preventing the sovereign from uniting and stabilizing the whole of the territory of Morocco. Such unification was achieved in a different manner, by the scholars of the law (or *'ulama*), on the one hand, and by the network of sanctuaries built by the Sufi brotherhoods, on the other. Both will be considered later in this chapter.

THE CITIES

The two most important cities in the Morocco of Mulay Ahmad al-Mansur were Fez, which had been the capital city of the Marinids until the mid-fifteenth century, and Marrakesh, capital of the south, founded by the Almoravids in the eleventh century.

Fez and Marrakesh

Fez, the oldest city in Morocco, was founded by the first Muslim dynasty of the region in the period immediately following the Arab conquest. A populous and well-organized city with a great tradition of religious learning, it was a hub of scholars and jurists, and one of the most important cities in the whole of the Islamic West. The call to prayer was made from hundreds of mosques, among which the centuries-old Qarawiyyin was the most celebrated. Students from the whole of North Africa flocked to its professors, lectures and rich library. The Marinids founded centres of higher education in Fez (*madrasas*), where grammar, rhetoric, theology and law were taught to the intellectual elites who supported the dynasty. To the west of the old, medieval city, the Marinids also founded New Fez (Fas Jadid) as a centre of government with palaces, barracks, stables and bazaars. The city welcomed traders to its markets from the surrounding region, who brought textiles, metalwork, food and gold, slaves and ivory from the caravans that crossed the Sahara from the Western Sudan. The city of Fez was proud of its citizens and its intellectual traditions. It was the virtual capital of northern Morocco and its people mistrusted everything that came from the south, which they regarded as barbarous and uncivilized.

Marrakesh, the capital of the south, was the city through which caravan traffic and trade with the southern Sahara was controlled. It had been the capital of the two Berber dynasties – the Almoravids and the Almohads – that had arisen to the south of the Atlas mountain range; both based their authority on rigorous, reforming religious preaching. The rivalry between Fez and Marrakesh, the disagreements between their intellectual schools and between the territories controlled by both cities, was constant throughout the early modern period. The two cities were even perceived at times as separate national entities in European documents, which refer to them as 'the kingdom of Fez' and 'the kingdom of Marrakesh'. Under the Sa'dian dynasty, also from the south of Morocco and thus more attached to Marrakesh, its capital, the post of governor of Fez was in practice a sort of viceroyship reserved for the heir to the throne. Muley Ahmad al-Mansur appointed his oldest son, Muley al-Shaykh, to the post of governor of the city just as he had been appointed to the same post by his brother Abd al-Malik.

The caravan traffic had been almost totally cut off from the sea by the Iberian forces' occupation of the most important ports on both the Mediterranean and Atlantic coasts of Morocco. However, a few strongholds remained in Moroccan hands, which were to become increasingly important during Ahmad's reign.

Salé

Located at the mouth of the river Bou Regreg, and now forming part of Rabat, this small, well-fortified city was initially populated by Andalusians. It soon became a refuge for corsairs. The sandbar outside the entrance to its port prevented large ships from entering, whereas the small, agile vessels used by the corsairs were able to take cover there. Throughout the reign of Ahmad al-Mansur, Salé grew in importance, but it was not until the seventeenth century, when the Moriscos were expelled from Spain, that the city became a corsair republic similar in extent and character to the Regency of Algiers. Salé gradually became an important port which handled most of Morocco's maritime trade.

Tetouan

Tetouan was similar in many ways to Salé. It was founded by natives of Granada exiled on the Mediterranean coast of Morocco under the leadership of Ali al-Manzari. Celebrated for his military feats against the Spaniards just before the conquest of Granada, al-Manzari rebuilt the fortress and town of Tetouan previously destroyed by the Portuguese, and used it as a base of operations against Portuguese Ceuta and Tangier, putting to good use the nearby port of Martil. In the sixteenth century, Tetouan was sustained by corsair activity and by attacking settlements on the coasts of the Iberian Peninsula to sack them, to take captives and, above all, to assist the Muslims still living in Spain (the Moriscos) to leave the country. By contrast with Salé, Tetouan's role diminished throughout the seventeenth century.

Another small port, Safi, on the southern Atlantic coast, also gained importance as the nearest sea port to Marrakesh. It was far from the commercial routes and therefore was not privileged by corsairs.

For Morocco, corsair activity was one of the few ways it could create a role for itself on the commercial circuit. In the long term, however, it was a deeply negative trend for the country. Neither industry nor wealth was created. Local shipyards were never established, nor arsenals founded. Ships were obtained through capture, supplies were brought from abroad and proper institutions were never created for the exploitation of the trade in ransomed captives.

This was partly due to the difficulties Morocco had in supplying itself with wood, iron, sail canvas and gunpowder. The Catholic countries of southern Europe were prohibited by Papal bull from selling to Muslim lands any materials that might be used to make war

against Christians, and Morocco was forced to turn for these products to Protestant countries unaffected by the ban, such as England
and Holland. But the fact is that corsair activity did not enrich the
local population for long and it brought few benefits to the Moroccan
dynasty. It did not establish links with a hinterland that could supply
or exploit corsair activity. It did not create an integrated economy or
society, and in fact served only to weaken social bonds. Corsair activity in Morocco was mainly conducted by foreigners who had settled
in the country, especially English and Dutch sailors, or by members
of the two groups of Moroccan society which were not, in Ahmad al-
Mansur's time, completely integrated in it: the Moriscos (or
Andalusians) and the Renegades to be considered in next chapter.

Common factors as well as the central feature of urban society
were the scholars of the law, the *'ulama*.

THE *'ULAMA*

The *'ulama* (singular *'alim*) were scholars of the Islamic sciences of
theology, Qur'anic studies, Prophetic tradition and religious law.
Their role was the interpretation of the Scriptures to obtain a ruling
upon any aspect of human life, worship, inheriting, marrying, buying
and selling, possessing, stealing, killing . . . They handed down their
wisdom from master to pupil, so that the authenticity of the faith
from the times of the Prophet to the present day was guaranteed. For
this transmission, book-learning was not enough: it was necessary to
have direct contact with the masters of the various disciplines, as
teaching and learning were based on the personal relationship
between master and disciple. Teaching took place mainly at mosques,
but also at professors' houses, and at state-funded institutions – the
madrasas – where students came to live and work with their teachers.
Travel was important for study, as students had to visit the most rep-
utable professors in their disciplines, and sit and read with them.
Moroccan students travelled to the East, in search of learning, especially to the holy cities of Mecca and Medina, but also to Cairo and

Alexandria. Thus, the *'ulama* represented not only an aspect of internal intellectual and legal cohesion in Morocco, but also a conduit through which Moroccan society was linked to and integrated with intellectual trends in the Middle East.

The most important step in a student's accreditation as a scholar in religious sciences was to be recognized as a link in a chain of transmission of learning through his professors and to be permitted to have his own students, in other words, to be part of a generational network. Unbroken chains of transmission of knowledge were considered reliable and were a source of legitimacy and power. Ahmad al-Mansur took care to have his scholarly *isnad* established: a chain of teachers and teachers of teachers that guaranteed the uninterrupted transmission of knowledge from the early Islamic generations and located Ahmad in a particular intellectual 'family' of scholars. His *isnad* was traced back to Muslim (d. 875), one of the most important early compilers of Prophetic traditions, and he sent it to Cairo for validation by one of the most respected scholars of the time, the master Abu 'l-Hassan al-Bakri.

In addition to knowledge, the *'ulama* also transmitted norms of behaviour, social and professional practices, and status. They tended to marry among themselves: it was not unusual for the brilliant disciple to marry the daughter of his teacher. Through the chains of transmission or *isnad,* the scholars created a genealogy of sorts, not especially through bonds of blood but through moral obligations of loyalty, dependence and self-support. That is precisely why Ahmad was interested in having his own *isnad* recorded and validated: he wished to show that he was an *'alim* and that he possessed a prestigious, scholarly pedigree.

Once they had completed their education and travels to acquire a proper pedigree, students returned home, where they became judges, administrators and notaries. They provided legal opinions on what was legal and legitimate and what was not, and decided how precedent or custom became law. They determined how holy texts should be interpreted, understood and implemented. Scholars also sought to participate as interpreters of the law on the political stage, where they played the role of counsel and arbiter, providing legitimization for political agendas. Theirs was the authority that backed measures taken by the politically powerful, through their knowledge of jurisprudence in applying the law. They had a very important political role in the ceremony of the *bay'a* , the solemn oath of allegiance that expressed the primordial relationship between the sultan and his subjects. At the outset of each new regime, the community, represented by the *'ulama*, swore allegiance to the candidate of its choice. This oath of allegiance, renewed every year on the great Muslim feast days, constituted an unbreakable bond between the people and the sultan established through the *'ulama*. The *'ulama* were central not only to the society of the city, but also to the politics of the state: their approval or disapproval was vital to the legitimation of the government and its policies in the eyes of the people.

The *'ulama* were not involved in the enforcement of the law, which was a matter of the sultan. For this purpose the sultan was assisted by the *qadi*, an official originally appointed and chosen among the *'ulama* to judge on behalf of the ruler in all matters within the community of the faithful. The *qadi* was a very important figure endowed with political power.

Two centuries earlier, the Marinid dynasty had established *madrasas* funded and controlled by the state with the objective of forming their own class of clerics and administrators, as well as ensuring their loyalty by controlling what was taught and by whom. It is also at these institutions that secretaries (*kuttab*) were trained. The education of these scribes required many years in the *madrasa*, as well as initiation into calligraphy and the manners of the palace. Unlike military personnel, these civil servants were relatively rare and, as we have seen, highly appreciated by the sultan. The closer, more personal relationship the military men maintained with the sovereign could undergo radical changes; as relatives or clients they did not hesitate to participate in factional struggles and to accumulate or seize new positions. But Ahmad al-Mansur's secretaries were faithful and extremely important for the construction of the sultan's power and legitimacy.

The role of the *'ulama* in Morocco was not really specific to the country, and was the same role played by their colleagues in Egypt or Syria. The role of the Sufi brotherhoods, on the other hand, was more specific to the Maghreb and one of the most important features of the period.

In the times immediately preceding the turn of the sixteenth century, two major developments took place which came to fruition during Ahmad al-Mansur's reign and were decisive for the political, religious and cultural history of Morocco until modern times. The first was the institutionalization of Sufism in corporatized brotherhoods associated with different 'paths' (*tariqa*) in the mystical life. These brotherhoods organized themselves, arranged their own hierarchies and established practices and rituals that distinguished them from each other. Codes were created to regulate the initiation of new members and their comportment.

The second feature, closely connected with the institutionalization of Sufism, is the prestige acquired by *sharif* (plural *shurafa* or *chorfa* in Moroccan Arabic), the descendants of the family of the Prophet Muhammad and the pre-eminence to which they rose in political and religious arenas, becoming a sort of blood aristocracy.

We need to take a closer look at these two features because of their importance for the kind of power that Ahmad al-Mansur had – with whom he was forced to share power, who made the decisions, who supported or rejected his decisions, and what forces he could rely upon to implement them. During the sixteenth century, Sufi lodges and their networks, disciplined groups of initiates, fortresses, palaces, tribes with their leaders, called *amghar* in Berber or *shaykhs* in Arabic, constituted the centres of power in the countryside.

THE SUFI BROTHERHOODS

Sufism, the mystical path of Islam, had existed for centuries. Unlike Islamic scholars, experts in the law and its interpretation, the Sufis aspired to closeness with God through divine intuition, inspiration and illumination, through both specific religious practices and spiritual training. Sufis offered, above all, the possibility of a different kind of religious knowledge, and they sought to break the monopoly that the *'ulama* had established over interpretation of the religious canon. In contrast to the scholars, Sufis were holy men who became known as *awliya* or 'friends [of God]' or saints. Sanctity, thus understood, was indicated by prodigies and supernatural events that confirmed a superhuman nature. The *awliya* were believed to be endowed with *baraka,* the blessing or grace of God. Sainthood, or the question of how God touches human beings, was not only a theological matter. It epitomized vitally important cultural and political dimensions because it called into play the very nature of knowledge and the boundaries of political authority.

Until about the thirteenth century, there had been isolated cases of mystics who enjoyed great reputations and left behind significant bodies of written work. These men were usually followed by scattered and disorganized generations of disciples. It was only from the fifteenth century onward that fully organized and corporatized schools were created and began to exercise great influence in Morocco, first in the rural areas and then in the cities. Like the orthodox scholars, the leaders or *shaykhs* of these brotherhoods also sought a role for themselves in the world of politics by supporting or discrediting figures in power and acting as arbiters in disputes, a role they were able to assume because of their alleged direct contact with God. To this end, they sought to develop characteristics that would associate them with prophets and prophecy, and thus with the greatest prophet of them all, Muhammad.

Each Sufi brotherhood was based at a *zawiya* or Sufi lodge, a sanctuary generally built around the tomb of the founder or *shaykh* of that brotherhood. The religious figures living in these lodges, or heading them, were popularly known as *murabitun* or marabouts. The sanctuaries were used as places of prayer and for the initiation of novices, but also served as places of pilgrimage, and shelters for the lawless who, in practice, were often rebels against political authorities. Their *shaykhs* mediated in conflicts among the local population or between the local population and representatives of the *makhzen* (the royal palace), and they were guarantors of peace in times of conflict in those areas where rival tribes came together to trade. They arbitrated in conflicts and guarded the caravanserais for the sub-Saharan trade and the way-stations of the caravan routes. The lodges were used as granaries and storehouses where peasants could store their crops to keep them safe from predators, including tax collectors. *Zawiyas* represented their communities in disputes and took responsibility for alleviating the periodic problems of hunger or drought.

QADIRIYYA AND SHADHILIYYA

Sufi brotherhoods identified themselves by the name of their founder. In late sixteenth-century Morocco, there were two brotherhoods of particular importance: the Qadiriyya, founded by a *sharif* from Iraq called Abd al-Qadir al-Jilani, and the Shadhiliyya, founded by the Moroccan *sharif* al-Shadhili. In Morocco, the Qadiriyya brotherhood brought to its own peculiar version of Sufi mysticism a series of pre-Islamic beliefs such as the worship of hidden, underground powers associated with caves, holy stones and a belief in the *jinn* or genies. The miraculous happenings, thaumaturgical powers, and rituals involving long fasts or sleep deprivation that were characteristic of the Qadiriyya were viewed with suspicion by many other Sufis. Some of the *'ulama*, especially the urban scholars, who were suspicious of even moderate mysticism, were alarmed by the extremes of these groups, and it is true that the worship of stones, caves, trees and holy places and other extreme forms of Sufism spread most widely in rural areas. This phenomenon has led some scholars to try to trace a division between 'rural Islam' and 'city Islam'. However, the sixteenth century saw the growing appeal of the mystical brotherhoods to urban scholars, and their growing involvement with the second great order, the Shadhiliyya.

The Shadhiliyya, a more 'moderate' path in its practices and ritual, had a great appeal for many *'ulama*. This brought about what might be described as a merger between those orthodox scholars and learned men who felt the attraction of Sufism, and those mystics who were disturbed by the excesses of some Sufi brotherhoods. This important development led to the overlapping of two – in theory – opposed paths to knowledge: on the one hand, erudite book-learning, and, on the other, intimacy with God through initiation, inspiration and prayer. Sufism was turning into a discipline that attracted the learned, including a number of high-ranking figures at court. The dynastic authorities used sanctification as an instrument of control and neutralization. In fact, a branch of the Shadhiliyya, the Jazuliyya, assisted the Sa'dians in their rise to power. Thus it was that sovereigns resorted to the protection of particular holy men, embellishing their graves and creating *ziyaras* or ritual visits in a sort of 'canonization' conferred by the dynasty on specific places and saints. Significantly, sultan Muley Ahmad would visit great shrines in person and, like his subjects, pray at the tombs of illustrious saints with regularity.

From the early thirteenth century on, the manifestation of divine power through privileged individuals can be said to have imbued the whole territory of the Maghreb with an aura of sanctity. Individual paths towards sainthood were gradually turned into axes of attraction which began to create a new map of veneration wherein particular sanctuaries and graves comprised a network or web uniting the territory of Morocco. A link was established between sainthood and specific geographical locations, and holy places were expected to be perpetuated by descendants of the saints concerned. In this way, sacred lineages were created which increasingly sought to vindicate their membership in the family of the Prophet. It was, moreover, an important factor of cohesion between the territories and peoples of Morocco.

The *zawiyas* or Sufi lodges founded their own dynasties. Sufi *shaykhs* became leading actors on the political stage, where they embodied the values of specific social groups such as peasants, urban artisans, outcasts or the impoverished. They were deeply involved in the spread and protection of agriculture. The attraction to saintly *shaykhs* revealed a general desire for peace and the unsullied execution of power, and was the source of a sense of community in rural areas. As champions of the struggle against injustice, the *shaykhs* went beyond their purely religious role to make themselves spokesmen for attitudes of rebellion against political power and against the strict supervision of orthodoxy by the *'ulama*. They embodied new forms of domination and submission, and they had the capacity to punish others, exercising both symbolic and physical violence.

They penetrated the field of political power in many different ways. Most importantly, some provided the founders of the Sa'dian dynasty with its initial impulse: *shaykhs* of the Jazuliyya brotherhood from the Sus region recruited troops from among the tribes, organized the funds necessary to arm them, preached in favour of the Sa'dians and fought alongside them in battle. They also took sides in the struggles for succession, by supporting one candidate or another. Abu 'l-Mahasin Yusuf al-Fasi, *shaykh* of the Shadhiliyya, fought in the battle of Alcazar beside Abd al-Malik as a way of displaying the brotherhood's support against his rival's claims to the throne. Other *murabitun* fought on the side of Muhammad al-Mutawakkil, the dethroned sultan. The variety of roles that could be played by these holy figures can also be seen in the embassy that Sultan Abdallah, Muley Ahmad's older brother, sent to Suleyman the Magnificent in Istanbul, headed by a well-known *murabit* from a *zawiya* in the region of the Dra'a.

Although it was a period when some scholars of the law, the *'ulama*, were attracted to Sufism and joined Sufi brotherhoods, the presence of both groups in the political arena led to rivalries, confrontations and arguments as to their respective capacities to wield religious authority. The *'ulama* insisted on their knowledge of the law and their capacity to interpret it. They saw themselves as the only actors enabled to dictate what was legitimate and illegitimate, moral and immoral, to define what was legal and illegal. The *'ulama* had been on the political stage for centuries, and continued to play an important role, holding posts in the judiciary and as *imams* of the mosques. Their role at the court was also influential: they could condone decisions taken by the sultan, or they could – and, in theory, should – rebuke him and argue against his decisions. Sharifism, to be considered next, was a means whereby the sultan could rise above both *'ulama* and *awliya*. Nevertheless debate and struggles over the question of moral authority and over the definition of the community were crucial during the period considered in this book.

SHARIFISM

The institutionalization of Sufism enhanced the phenomenon of 'Sharifism', the growing prestige and social hegemony of those who claimed to be *sharifs*, descendants of the Prophet Muhammad. To a certain extent, this phenomenon was also related to the major development mentioned above, the Arabization of the population and the perceived prestige of Arab lineages. The prestige of families claiming to be descendants of the Prophet had increased in Morocco for almost two hundred years, and was bolstered by a growing cult of the figure of the Prophet associated with the Sufis. However, the most outstanding feature of sharifism in the sixteenth century was the gradual consolidation of the idea that descent from the family of the Prophet (being *sharif*) was both a necessary and a sufficient prerequisite for wielding religious and political power. In this way, a blood aristocracy was formed that implicitly (and sometimes explicitly) carried with it the notion that some of the gifts of the Prophet (and even prophecy itself, a most heterodox belief) were hereditary. As the sixteenth century wore on, the *shaykhs* of all mystical brotherhoods began to claim a line of descent going back to the family of the Prophet. The post of *shaykh* of a brotherhood also started to become hereditary: a *shaykh* would tend to be the son of the previous *shaykh* rather than the disciple generally recognized as the most saintly or most brilliant. Dynasties of holy men thus created holy lineages that were identified with sharifism.

Important sharifian families acquired large landholdings by decree of the sovereign. The most respected ones received the *sila*, a kind of regular allowance in the form of a gift. They were exempted from taxes.

In sixteenth-century Morocco the Sharifian argument was force-fully invoked in the exercise of power and its legitimation. In the act of investiture, in the homilies that accompanied Friday prayers and in the rituals that marked the Muslim year, the presence of the *shurafa* provided an indispensable consecration. During the *bay'a*, the oath of allegiance to the sovereign, they were the first witnesses to be named because of the grace stemming from their genealogy. Nothing could be done without them. Indeed the *'ulama* were the custodians of the Prophet's teachings and tradition. The *shurafa* derived their primacy from the fact that their presence was a tangible manifestation of the Prophet's 'mystical body'.

The *shurafa* participated alongside the sultan in all great rituals. But it was in the annual celebration of the Prophet's birth, to be con-sidered later, that their ascendancy was at its most spectacular.

But what was the role of the military in these urban and rural elites? What place did the army and its members occupy in society?

THE ARMY

To back up his claim to authority, the sultan needed the power of the army. The army was recruited from the Arab tribes known as *jaysh / guish*, meaning those that provided men in the event of war. In exchange for their military services, these tribes were freed from taxation or granted lands that enabled them to levy taxes on local populations. The *guish* tribes were potentially dangerous for the sov-ereign, as they were liable to change sides during rivalries and dis-putes for the throne. The army had also, besides the *jaysh* tribes, a standing core that lived in barracks and whose troops were known as *al-makhzaniya*, i.e. troops of the state, or *al-makhzen*. This standing army's members were paid a regular salary by the sultan, generally taken from his revenues from the sugar industry. The sultan's per-sonal guard was drawn from these troops; magnificently attired, they accompanied the sultan on caparisoned horses in parades and on offi-cial journeys, as well as on the battleground.

The standing army comprised light cavalry, a number of mounted matchlockmen or harquebusiers, and an infantry corps armed with rifles. The troops equipped with firearms were composed of foreign soldiers: Turks, Sudanese and, above all, Renegades and Moriscos. In cases of extreme necessity, such as Don Sebastian's invasion, these troops were increased by a draft of sedentary peoples of the plains and men from those cities whose loyalty was deemed reliable. Moroccan sultans avoided general conscription as far as possible – it was a last resort, because the sovereign feared handing power to the tribes by supplying them with firearms. There were two issues at work: reluctance to conscript the entire population, and reluctance to issue firearms to anyone except foreigners. The Maqil Arabs, for example, one of the *guish* tribes, were equipped with chain-mail armour, helmets, antelope shields, sabres and five-metre spears, but were never allowed the use of firearms. Ahmad al-Mansur had no desire to supply such dangerous weapons to any group that might become involved in an uprising against him. Neither the Moriscos nor the Renegades were truly integrated in Moroccan society, and therefore they would have been unable to rely on the support of local followers in an armed revolt. On the contrary, they depended on the sultan completely. One of Ahmad al-Mansur's major worries throughout his reign, mentioned in several letters to his sons, was the matter of limiting the possession of firearms to those he could control and ensuring the loyalty of the tribes from whom his troops were recruited. On several occasions during his reign, Al-Mansur had to deal with the uprisings of various tribes that declared themselves in revolt against him, refusing to pay taxes, and rejecting his authority. The sultan was wary and always vigilant of the power of his own military officials. Diego de Torres describes in his chronicle the arrival in Marrakesh of the governor of Tagaost, from the south, a reputed and powerful *shaykh* of this region. Torres himself followed the *shaykh* and his retinue on his way to the mosque: he was a man of about ninety years of age (meaning very old), tall, dark and meagre, grave, full of dignity and poise, 'representing very well what he was'. He marched accompanied by sixty-six men, all of whom were his sons and grandsons, all of them riding beautifully caparisoned horses, wearing silks of all colours and capes of Florentine purple, with quivers and boxes for their swords plated in gold. It was a very impressive spectacle, Torres remarks, and adds that he considered it a very wise measure when, as he heard a few days later, the sultan had transferred this *shaykh* up to the north, to Alcazar, away from his social bases.

The preponderance of cavalry in the Moroccan army gave it great mobility and ease of manoeuvre. Even the light artillery, which took the form of low-calibre cannons, was transported by mules. Some of the army corps rode on camels, which were also used to transport the heavier cannons. In mountainous territories, where it was difficult for the animals to carry cannons, army members took metal components with them in order to reconstruct the cannons as and where they were needed. Ahmad al-Mansur's army also had a magnificent medical service, with surgeons and barbers accompanying the army on campaign equipped with their own hospital tents, ointments, medicine, dressings for bandages and so on.

In fact, the sixteenth century saw the gradual substitution of an army based on tribal formations by a professional army essentially made up of foreign elements that were not fully integrated in Moroccan society. Thus, a career in the army never became prestigious, and its officers had a fairly low status in civil society. Military careers were not linked to the possession of land or its transmission by hereditary means. Despite the considerable power achieved by many army officers, they did not establish ties through marriage with the families of *'ulama* or *shurafa*. The elites of the realms of knowledge, science and the law had very little to do with the military classes.

Before passing to the description of the role of the Renegades, Moriscos and Jews in Ahmad's government, it is necessary to have in mind a brief description of his Ottoman-style regime based on the model already established by his brother Abd al-Malik, but central to Ahmad's effort. First in the hierarchy after the sultan was the *wazir* or vizier, a post generally given to the crown prince, in fact a viceroy.

The First Secretary was the head of the sultan's council and had competences as secretary of state, majordomo and treasurer. The vizier had a vice-vizier in charge of the army and of his higher officers, who included the other sons of the sultan, brothers and relatives who had command over the cavalry, the forces endowed with firearms and the personal guard of the sultan. The judiciary was headed by the main qadi (qadi al-qudat), who appointed qadis to different cities and regions. The sultan appointed officers for tax recollection. They moved in the court together with a series of caballeros, says Diego de Torres, who had lands and castles given by the king for his sustenance and accompanied him in peace and war. Among them the sultan chose the members of his privy council. In this council there was a chancellor of the seal (whose responsibilities were letters, documents, treaties), a member dedicated to protocol and ceremonies, a member in charge of the horses and camels of the sultan, and a member dedicated to the administration and division of rents and taxes. The sultan had also private counsellors and persons close to him because of their upbringing or through personal trust. Many of them belonged to the categories considered in the next chapter.

4

RENEGADES, MORISCOS
AND JEWS

Renegades, Moriscos and Jews played a prominent role in the Morocco of Ahmad al-Mansur. They were, in fact, the extension of the sultan's power, representing his army, his guard, the crews of his corsair ships, his treasury officials and tax collectors and the protagonists of his main economic and commercial programmes. Nonetheless, they were marginalized by Moroccan society, were never truly integrated and never formed part of the elite despite the military and economic power that many of them achieved. It was precisely because they were outsiders that they served in those roles. If they came to be integrated they ceased being useful precisely because dynasty officials were meant not to represent society.

It must be admitted, however, that the apparent imbalance between this sector of society and the one discussed in the previous chapter – the Muslim *'ulama* and *sharifs* – is accentuated by the source material: Arabic sources deal primarily with scholars, saints and *sharifs* either in hagiographic compendiums, biographical dictionaries of *'ulama*, or genealogical works on Arab and *sharif* lineages, while European documents are mainly concerned with the groups with whom foreign merchants, agents and diplomatic envoys had dealings: precisely the groups under consideration here.

RENEGADES

The conflict in the Mediterranean, fought mainly between the Ottomans and the Habsburgs, but also including Venice, produced an extraordinary number of captives. After the 1570s, great naval battles were no longer fought, but the trade in ransomed captives was kept alive by what Braudel called 'la petite guerre' – that is, corsair warfare, as discussed in the previous chapter. It was a secondary form of war, another way of fighting the battle between Christianity and Islam, at least in theory, since the true stakes were economic. From along the southern Mediterranean coast from Tripoli to Tetouan, and from the Atlantic ports of Larache and Salé, Muslim corsair ships were a constant threat to the coasts, ships and trading routes of the northern Mediterranean countries. The 'corsair war' reached its apex between 1580 and 1640; its main centre of operation was the Turkish regency of Algiers established by the Barbarossa brothers in 1518.

One of the main objectives of corsair warfare was human booty, and an entire ransom industry was built around recovering it. The religious orders of the Trinitarians and the Mercedarians traversed the Catholic countries of the northern Mediterranean seeking alms to finance the payment of such ransoms. The captives themselves were employed as labourers in public works (such as the construction of ports and shipyards), as domestic servants in wealthy households, and at the royal courts of corsair cities while awaiting liberation.

An indeterminate but considerable number of captives chose to change their status by converting to Islam. These converts were characteristic of sixteenth- and seventeenth-century Mediterranean society, and were referred to in Arabic as the *uluj* (singular *ilj*) and in Spanish and other Christian sources as *elches* or *renegados*, 'those who deny [their faith]'. Conversions were made for various reasons, not only spiritual persuasion: despair of ever being ransomed, the rigours of physical mistreatment, the desire to regain personal freedom, and the attraction of integration into Islamic society. Those who were taken captive tended to be from the peasant classes of the poorest regions of the Christian Mediterranean, areas such as Calabria, Sicily, southern Spain and Provence. The Muslim societies of North Africa, socially less rigid than the captives' countries of origin, allowed them to make fortunes quickly, and Europeans were able to reach social positions there that would have been unthinkable in their native lands. The religious frontier in the Mediterranean was weak, rather porous and easily overcome, and admittance into Islam was relatively simple as there were no institutions that controlled beliefs to question a new convert's sincerity or fulfilment of religious obligations. All that was needed to convert to Islam was to raise one finger (a sign that there is only one God), pronounce the *shahada* (the testimony of faith), change one's name and dress and submit to circumcision in the case of males. However, the names by which the Renegades were known (*ilj* or *elche*) reveal much about the limitations of their conversion to Islam.

In Morocco, most Renegades were of Spanish and Portuguese origin. As in other areas of North Africa, the Renegades constituted a caste, a closed social group forming part of a hierarchy with an important political and military role: they served in the personal guard of governors and of the sultan; they joined the army, government administrations, and, interestingly enough, the crews of corsair ships. In the seventeenth century the Renegades began to use larger northern ships that allowed them to sail together with English privateers beyond the Strait of Gibraltar and into the open sea.

Muslim society did not invigilate or control the Renegades, but it did confine them to their own political and social corner. There they lived as clients, related closely, even intimately, to their former masters or sovereign. Thus, conversion was linked to manumission, but also to the master–client relationship: Renegades maintained a client relationship with their former masters, who often found it more profitable to employ them as free converts than as slaves.

One prominent example of a successful renegade was Ridwan al-Ilj, chief of the personal guard of Sultan Abd al-Malik and later that of Ahmad al-Mansur, at whose court he played an important role. Ahmad al-Mansur had a corps of some four thousand Renegades in his army. His personal guard was composed mainly of Renegades, and large numbers were employed as servants in his palace, almost all Portuguese captives from the battle of Alcazar. Like Ridwan al-Ilj, some of these captives came to play leading roles at court as secretaries, translators and personal advisers.

ANDALUSIANS OR MORISCOS

The spectacular, and eventually definitive, advances of Christian troops into the Muslim kingdom of Granada from 1450 to 1492 forced its inhabitants into an exile that would decisively affect North Africa. The tide of emigration from the kingdom of Granada to Morocco reached a peak after Granada's fall in 1492, when the conditions for Muslims in the Peninsula changed dramatically. Until then, Muslims had been able, if they wished, to remain in their homes and to maintain their communal religion and laws under a statute that they, and the Jews, had enjoyed in the Peninsular Christian territories in various areas since the eleventh century. Now this no longer proved possible.

The fall of Granada marked the disappearance of the last Peninsular territory under Muslim rule. With this conquest, Ferdinand and Isabella, known as the Catholic Kings, unified the territory now known as Spain under the same crown, and undertook a series of measures to homogenize the territory in social and political terms. These included a unification of legal norms and religious beliefs. At the same time, the rights of the state to intervene in all facets of its subjects' political, social and religious life were augmented, and institutions were created (or imported) to carry out such control. The Inquisition is the most notorious example of such institutions. Spanish Jews were the first victims of this new state of affairs. They were obliged by the Catholic Kings to choose between exile and forced conversion to the Catholic faith. Most Jews left the country, many for Morocco or the Ottoman territories.

A decade later, in 1502, a similar decree was published, this time requiring the conversion of all Muslims living in the territories of the old kingdom of Castile, including the kingdom of Granada. Possibly haunted by the experience of the massive Jewish exodus in 1492, the Spanish monarchy offered a nominal choice between conversion and exile, but created conditions that made the second option all but impossible to exercise. The forcibly converted Muslims, known as Moriscos, were subjected to rigid social and economic control by the state and were repressed by the Inquisition. This time, the exodus towards the north of Africa from the towns near the southern coast of the Peninsula became a slow, permanent drip.

The monarchy perceived the Moriscos as a significant problem. The national ethos insisted vehemently on assimilation into Christian society, while simultaneously fearing that Muslim 'blood', and thus Islamic beliefs and Muslim cultural practices, would spread throughout the population. This contradiction was the source of many difficulties for the Moriscos. The decision was taken that all cultural practices associated with Muslims would have to be eradicated in order to speed the assimilation of Moriscos into Christian society. During the first half of the sixteenth century, the Spanish authorities undertook a series of measures designed to evangelize and catechize the Moriscos – a project that was later considered a failure.

In 1567 Philip II issued a decree declaring that the Moriscos of Granada were forbidden to use Arabic, spoken or written, to possess books or documents written in Arabic – whatever their subject matter – and to employ Arabic names and surnames; traditional clothing was banned, and women were forbidden from covering any part of their face and from using henna to adorn their hands, feet or hair; Morisco music was prohibited at weddings and other celebrations; a ban was placed on the use of baths and the possession of slaves; and, finally, the Moriscos were ordered to keep the doors of their houses open permanently. The consternation caused by the decree was immense.

In response, in 1568, the war of the Alpujarras – the armed rebellion of the Moriscos in the Alpujarras mountains, stretching from

Granada to Almería – broke out. This cruel and bloody war lasted two years: the Moriscos were crushed towards the end of 1570. Philip II's victory was celebrated by the decision to deport all of the Moriscos from their lands in Granada to Castile in the north.

A considerable number of Moriscos fled to Morocco at this time. Known as 'Andalusians' in Morocco, they settled along the coasts, where they took to corsair activity or were recruited for the Moroccan army. Bellicose, rootless and accustomed to handling firearms – which was uncommon in Morocco at that time – they were predictably bitter towards the Spanish authorities that had persecuted them in the Peninsula. As Iberian natives, they had good knowledge of the Peninsular languages and of the geography of the coastal regions, which made their corsair incursions particularly dangerous for the Spanish.

Throughout North Africa, the Moriscos and the Renegades were engaged in similar occupations, and had similar skill sets, factors that made them difficult to distinguish from one another. They lived in the same areas, took on the same trades and professions, fought together on the same corsair ships or in the militias and personal guards of governors and were employed as translators and secretaries. For almost a century, both groups found resistance to their full integration into Moroccan society.

The Moriscos found that their status as Muslims was ambiguous: many spoke Spanish and not Arabic as their mother tongue, a product of their long years of forced conversion and repression in Spain. Expelled from their homeland, they were regarded with suspicion in their new domicile. Many Andalusian exiles complained bitterly about their situation: they could scarcely earn their livelihood in Morocco and wished only to return to Granada. These complaints did not endear them to Moroccan society: rather, the learned jurist Ahmad al-Wansharisi from Fez wrote legal responses (*fatwas*) rebuking them for their weakness of faith.

Sultan Abdallah, Ahmad's eldest brother, reigned in Morocco at the time of the war of the Alpujarras. The positive diplomatic relations he had established with Philip II made him reluctant to provide the Morisco rebels with the military aid and food they requested. He did, however, give assistance and shelter to the exiled Moriscos who arrived in his country. In particular, he gave them land in the plains outside Marrakesh, where they created water-powered mills and vegetable gardens irrigated by a system of channels that brought water down from the Atlas mountains. These measures helped the Moriscos, according to Arabic sources, to assuage the nostalgia they felt for their homeland. Some of them settled down as peasants, gardeners and agricultural labourers. Both on the plains of Marrakesh and in the region between the cities of Fez and Meknes, the Moriscos planted white mulberry trees for the breeding of silkworms, sericulture being an industry in which Muslims and Moriscos specialized in Spain. They were also skilled artisans and craftsmen, carpenters and masons, often specializing in plastering, roofing and tile work. They found ample employment in Ahmad al-Mansur's major building projects in Marrakesh, his capital city. They also took part in the construction of the sugar mills and refineries that Ahmad al-Mansur built in the Sus region. Many also left Marrakesh for Salé with permission to equip ships as privateers, and set out to sea.

Sultan Abdallah drafted newly arrived Moriscos to create an artillery corps that he placed under the command of al-Dugali, a Morisco from Granada. The sources claim that al-Dugali gathered as many as fourteen thousand of his compatriots in this corps, but the figure seems slightly exaggerated. In the years that followed, there is evidence for a corps of Andalusian artillerymen comprising 2000–5000 men – depending on the occasion – who were highly skilled in the use of the harquebus. Abdallah's draft was compulsory and extremely unpopular among the Andalusians, many of whom would no doubt have preferred to continue to devote themselves to the practice of irrigated agriculture as they had in Spain.

In Spain, the rebellious Moriscos received no assistance from Morocco, and resorted to sending representatives to Istanbul to request military aid. The Ottomans sent them a number of soldiers and some equipment from Algiers. Two of the Morisco representatives sent to Istanbul are well-known figures, who made contact there with Abd al-Malik, then a pretender to the Moroccan throne. The most important of these, Muhammad Zarqun, became a close friend of Abd al-Malik, and later was his majordomo and main adviser. News of defeat in the Alpujarras arrived while the envoys were in Istanbul, and Abd al-Malik asked them instead to help him form an artillery corps. He provided them with equipment and money – again in the form of precious stones – to enter Morocco and make contact with their compatriots, including al-Dugali and his troops. Abd al-Malik was accompanied by the Morisco envoys on their return journey to Algiers.

We have already seen how contacts came into play: in 1576, when Abd al-Malik returned to Morocco accompanied by a Turkish army to fight against his nephew Muhammad, al-Dugali's Andalusian troops (which Muhammad inherited from his father) went over to the side of the candidate supported by the Turks. This defection illustrates how strongly the Moriscos identified the Turks as their allies and possible saviours. It also demonstrates that the Moriscos found Abdallah's refusal to help the Muslims of the Alpujarras unforgivable. It was this battle that opened the gates of Fez to Abd al-Malik.

Abd al-Malik sent the Turkish troops who had come with him back to Algiers, and formed his own personal guard of six thousand harquebusiers, one-third of whom were Renegades and the other two-thirds Andalusians. Both groups were ideally suited to this kind of work. That they were not truly Moroccan and were not linked to tribes or groups with aspirations to political power guaranteed their dependence on the sovereign and their loyalty to him. Towards the Moroccan population, on the other hand, and at least in principle, they preserved a certain neutrality.

Abd al-Malik also restructured his army by forming troops within it based on the ethnic and geographical background of members; among them, he was careful to form and train other units of harquebusiers or matchlockmen. The Andalusians' loss of the monopoly over such work did not sit well with their commanders, now known as 'bashas' or 'pashas' in line with the Turkish terminology preferred by Abd al-Malik.

The fact that there was no separation between civil and military administrations meant that these pashas, and figures like al-Dugali, became virtual governors of their own provinces, exercising administrative and fiscal power at a local level. Tax collection was carried out under the threat and protection of the pashas' armies, and this gave them great power. They were the 'king's men' in the provinces, with responsibility for tax collection from local communities and tribes in the course of tax-collecting expeditions. Muhammad Zarqun remained close to Abd al-Malik and played a role equivalent to that of a vizier, effectively the sovereign's prime minister.

Abd al-Malik did not eliminate his nephew Muhammad in their first battle and Muhammad fled, taking refuge in the interior of the country. During the months of war that followed, Muley Ahmad and al-Dugali were given the task of leading the military campaign against him. The Andalusians were firmly convinced that Abd al-Malik owed his rise to their participation and support, and during these months of campaigning Muley Ahmad came to harbour deep suspicions about their ambitions and loyalty. Ahmad's close contact with the Morisco pashas meant that their views became known to him.

It seems that after the battle of Alcazar, al-Dugali and Muhammad Zarqun planned to take control of Marrakesh and dethrone Ahmad, now proclaimed sultan. Other Andalusian pashas loyal to the sultan warned Ridwan al-Ilj (the Portuguese renegade who captained the sultan's guard) of the danger. Ahmad al-Mansur dispatched against these rebels the alternative artillery corps thoughtfully nurtured by his brother. These corps defeated the rebels, delivered the heads of both leaders to Ahmad and confiscated the rebels' money, equipment and weapons. Other Andalusian pashas were executed in Fez at the same time. However, even these measures did not end the pre-eminence of the Andalusian troops. They still had an important role to play during Ahmad's rule, as we will see during his conquest of Sudan.

Moriscos were also employed at court, including well-known figures such as Ahmad ben Qasim al-Andalusi, known as al-Hajari, secretary and translator to Ahmad and later to his son Muley Zidan. Al-Hajari wrote an interesting description of the journey he made to France and Holland on an official mission for the sultan. He also translated a number of religious works from Arabic to Spanish for the use of exiled Moriscos who had not yet learnt Arabic. In Tunis, towards the end of his life, al-Hajari translated a specialized manual on artillery from Spanish into Arabic.

There were other figures who provided valuable services as translators and interpreters, such as Sidi Abdala Dodar, a Morisco 'andalouz being borne in Granada' who spoke good Spanish and some Italian, and accompanied members of the Moroccan embassy to England in 1600 as an interpreter. Ahmad al-Mansur had another Andalusian interpreter, Abd al-Rahman al-Kattani, who in 1609 makes an appearance in the chronicles as Muley Zidan's translator in Marrakesh. Moriscos including Ahmad ibn Abdallah al-Maruni and Yusuf Biscaino also became ambassadors to England and to Holland.

JEWS

As mentioned above, in 1492 Spanish Jews were subject to a royal decree that required them to choose between expulsion and conversion to Catholicism. The vast majority opted for exile. Spain was the penultimate European country to expel its Jewish population (the last being Portugal); Jews were expelled from every other nation of Europe during the medieval period. After 1492, Jews were forced to take refuge in Portugal or in the lands of Islam.

In Morocco, as in the Ottoman Empire and in Islamic society in general, Jews were accommodated in Muslim society by means of the so-called '*dhimma* pact'. This pact awarded them status as protected people, allowing them (and Christians) to preserve their religion and law, and to retain their communal authorities and relative independence, though always in a state of submission and subjection. The statute was similar to that which had governed Jewish and Muslim communities in the medieval Christian kingdoms of the

Iberian Peninsula. According to the *dhimma* pact, Jews could not hold positions of power or superiority over Muslims. In sixteenth-century Morocco, however, many Jewish families were powerful, wealthy and held positions of power in government. These positions were highly vulnerable, and depended on the personal will of the sovereign. Historians such as Leo Africanus described Jewish soldiers hired by tribal chieftains as carrying arms and riding on horses, both activities that clearly contradict the *dhimma* regulations.

Since the end of the medieval period, the persecutions inflicted upon Jews in Spain and Portugal had encouraged messianic and apocalyptic expectations among them. To Jews harassed by Christians, or at least to some of them, Islam assumed a providential role, especially after the Muslim conquest of Constantinople. In the struggle between the Christian West and the Muslim Turkish East, some Jews saw the signs of their own liberation, and the dawn of a messianic era. Thus, the spectacular scale of the emigration of expelled Jews to the Middle East and North Africa was motivated not only by the opportunity offered by the Islamic world to practise their religion freely, but also by messianic ideas about Islam's future as the triumphant vanquisher of the Christians. This sort of identification was still apparent in Morocco in 1578, after the defeat of Don Sebastian at Alcazar: the Jews of Fez and Tetouan celebrated the defeat, and established a *Purim* (a festival expressing satisfaction and gratitude after the dissolution of a threat of destruction) that has been celebrated ever since until recent times.

In Portugal, the presence of Jews was still legal in 1492. However, circumstances soon became even tougher there than in Spain. King Don Manoel I imposed forced conversion on the Jews in 1497, removing the option of exile. These Portuguese 'New Christians' and their descendants were not allowed to leave the country even after they had been baptized, and thus crypto-Jews came to form a coherent, unshakeable and active force in Portugal.

In 1536, King João III introduced the Inquisition to Portugal, where the Holy Office devoted all its efforts to the repression of 'judaizing' practices and beliefs among the New Christians. Concurrently, a slow, clandestine re-emigration back to Spain began among some Jews, just as New Christians fled to Portuguese territories overseas. The Portuguese strongholds in Morocco – Ceuta, Mazagan and Tangier – also saw significant numbers of Portuguese crypto-Jews fleeing repression; some managed to cross the frontier into Morocco, settling, above all, in the city of Fez.

Fez had had a large Jewish population since its foundation. Both the city and its Jewish minority had flourished from the thirteenth century onwards with the rise of the Marinids, who made Fez the capital of their kingdom and employed Jewish servants and administrators at court. As in medieval Christian Spain, popular animosity towards Jews tended to grow in proportion to the protection and favourable treatment they received from the monarch. For this reason, in the mid-fifteenth century, the entire Jewish population of Fez was removed to the new palatine city that the dynasty built for itself on the outskirts of the capital. In New Fez (Fas Jadid), the sultan established the first Jewish quarter in North Africa for the purpose of protecting Jews from the constant danger of popular riots against them. This quarter was created within a designated area known as the Mellah (Arabic *Mallah*, or 'salty soil'). The Mellah of Fez became a densely populated and renowned centre of Jewish life for the next century and a half. The term *mellah* became a synonym for a Jewish quarter throughout the whole of Morocco. Interestingly enough, Spanish sources referred to the Fez Mellah by the medieval Spanish term *judería* (the Spanish *juderías* had been established centuries earlier by Christian monarchs for similar reasons). It was not a walled ghetto, but rather a neighbourhood similar to the ones that foreign merchants established in Moroccan and other North African cities. Contemporary European observers left detailed descriptions of the Jewish quarter of Fez, which in the mid-sixteenth century contained as many as ten thousand householders, indicating a total population of forty or fifty thousand individuals, most of them of Spanish origin. This is an exaggerated estimate, indicating that the Jewish population was huge to contemporary eyes.

The Jewish quarter was also the area designated to receive all non-Muslim visitors to the city, including Christian travellers, ambassadors, commercial agents and, above all, captives waiting to be ransomed. After 1578, the Mellah of Fez was home to a particularly large number of Portuguese prisoners from the battle of Alcazar, who stayed in the Mellah while the demands for their ransom were met.

Procuring the ransom could take a considerable time. The Portuguese chronicler Jeronimo de Mendoça, himself a captive, described the Portuguese prisoners taken at Alcazar who were sent to the Mellah, writing that they were the luckiest of all the hostages because they were so well treated by the Jews, who 'mourned a thousand times their banishment from Spain.' At the same time, Mendoça explained that the Jewish hosts had neither the power nor the means to mistreat the captives, and that for the latter it was a great relief to be able to speak with these hosts 'because in general they speak Spanish.' Mendoça wrote that the Count of Vimioso, an apparently privileged Mellah captive, shared his house with a preaching friar, and the pair of them engaged in religious polemics with leading Jewish figures. According to Mendoça, the meetings were attended by as many as twenty or thirty rabbis, who listened and argued 'with much moderation and reasonableness.' From other Portuguese sources, we learn that the noblemen among the captives 'lived with as much opulence and splendour in the treatment of their persons as if they were lords of the land, and as well as having their own rooms in some very splendid homes belonging to the Jews, with expensive beds and tapestries, they spent very generously on clothing themselves in rich silks and on food, making greater expenditures than if they had been living at home in Portugal.' In order to meet these expenditures, the free-spending noblemen borrowed money from their Jewish hosts, or gave them letters of credit for loans to be paid off in Portugal.

The Jews of Fez who engaged in trades specialized in occupations that were either forbidden to the Muslim population, such as money-lending, or disdained by them, such as metalwork. They became jewellers, goldsmiths, minters of coins, arms manufacturers, and makers of special varieties of gold and silver braid. Fez reached the peak of its political and economic development in the mid-sixteenth century, when it was a powerful magnet for Jews hoping to work in trade, finance or administration. By the end of the century, Jews of Spanish origin were omnipresent in Moroccan foreign trade, administration and diplomacy.

Fez was also an important cultural and intellectual centre for both Muslims and Jews. Throughout the sixteenth century, Fez became a place of return to Judaism for crypto-Jews of Spanish and Portuguese origin, a place where they could acquire or regain Jewish culture and religious knowledge. For a number of years, there was even a Hebrew printing press in Fez. Intellectual standards in the Mellah seem to have been high during the mid-sixteenth century. Nicholas Clénard, a highly educated Flemish humanist and scholar who visited Fez with the aim of evangelizing among the Muslims, was impressed by the scholarship of many inhabitants of the Jewish quarter, where he stayed. Clénard was even able to find work for himself as a teacher of Latin, Greek and classical Arabic to Jewish students.

However, Fez fell behind when Ahmad al-Mansur made Marrakesh his capital. In the second half of the sixteenth century, many Jewish families that were linked to the court or the world of finance moved out of the Mellah of Fez to the new Moroccan capital. Two thousand Portuguese captives were also taken there from Fez, and foreign traders and diplomats on missions to the sultan began to go to Marrakesh instead of Fez.

The Spanish Jews who settled in Morocco brought with them not only the Spanish language, which they maintained, but also other types of expertise. They brought their libraries and the knowledge of administrative practices acquired by members of some families who had worked as scribes and fiscal and commercial agents at the courts of Aragon and Castile for centuries. They were able to draw upon this kind of expertise in Morocco. The presence of Morisco and Jewish translators, interpreters and diplomatic agents at the sultan's court was one of the reasons why Spanish became the language used in all official diplomatic business with Morocco during the sixteenth and seventeenth centuries.

Ahmad al-Mansur employed a Jewish financial adviser, Ya'qub Ruti, who was entrusted with diplomatic relations with Portugal and the ransom payments for Portuguese captives from the battle of Alcazar. Ransom negotiations were often made the responsibility of some of the numerous Jewish families living in Salé or Tetouan. Jews were also in charge of diplomatic relations between the Portuguese-controlled ports and Morocco, both in times of conflict and as part of habitual trading relations. In fact, Jews managed a substantial portion of Moroccan foreign trade, as the English and Dutch traders who sought to break this monopoly for their own gain frequently complained. Many Jews in foreign trade reached positions of economic power, and some of them, like Ruti, enjoyed considerable political influence. Moroccan Jews also administered the sugar cane refineries established by Ahmad al-Mansur in the regions of Sus and Tafilalt, and traded in sugar and molasses.

Before the successful competition of the West Indies and Brazil in the sugar industry, sugar cane was the most valuable Moroccan cash crop. The cultivation and refining of sugar cane had been prevalent in Morocco since the medieval period, but Muhammad al-Shaykh, Ahmad's father, greatly increased the number of plantations and applied Venetian methods of refining brought to Morocco by Andalusians and Christian captives. The cane plantations were the sultan's personal property. The sugar mills, called *ingenios de azucar* in Spanish records and *ingenewes* in English documents, were a monopoly of the dynasty and profits from them were funnelled into the state treasury. Both Moriscos and Christian captives were employed in them as labourers.

The importance of Moroccan sugar products can be gauged from a detailed account of the arrival of a caravan of camels, mules and horses in Oran in 1569, loaded with sugar and molasses from the 'kingdom of Fez', under the supervision of 'a very rich Jew' and a large number of Arab soldiers employed by him as protection from bandits. The cargo of 5000 *arrobas* (1 *arroba* = 13 kilos, approximately) was later transported to Spain because of its high quality and low price. Some years later, Sultan Abd al-Malik negotiated a deal with the English Barbary Company, according to the terms of which the Moroccans promised not to sell sugar to Spain or Portugal, so as to leave the sugar trade in the hands of English and Dutch merchants.

Two other Moroccan export products of high value were gold and copper. The gold came from the sub-Saharan regions, and the copper from Moroccan mines. Copper was also consumed internally for, among other things, the cauldrons in which the sugar was boiled. These two products required a significant network of caravan routes for their transportation to the ports, and this trade was almost completely managed by important Jewish merchants.

Groups of merchants from various European nations also lived in Moroccan ports and cities. Many remained in Morocco for periods of more than twenty years, sometimes for their entire lives. They inhabited separate neighbourhoods in the cities like the *mellahs*, and often established close relations with the locals, especially members of the court, who provided them with access to the sultan. Sometimes their loyalties to their home countries were tested by the authorities of their own nations. There is evidence, for example, in contemporary Spanish documents that Spanish and Portuguese merchants were frowned upon if they had lived too long in Morocco. The Duke of Medinasidonia often recommended in his correspondence with the Spanish king, or with the Spanish and Portuguese governors of Tangier or Ceuta, that these merchants should not be employed as informers or diplomatic agents. There is no way of knowing, he said, how people who had been cut off from Christian society for so long, who had not complied with religious obligations and ritual, and who had personal friendships in Morocco, would react in circumstances where their loyalties were put to the test. And they were put to test indeed when commerce and diplomacy were intertwined, as we will see in the next chapter.

5

DIPLOMACY AND TRADE

In the months following the battle of Alcazar, Ahmad al-Mansur was visited by emissaries from various countries. Among the first to arrive were the Portuguese and the Spanish. Al-Mansur treated them politely and with generosity: he handed over Don Sebastian's body and two prominent Portuguese noblemen without asking for ransom. Ahmad sent reports simultaneously to all of the neighbouring Muslim territories to inform them of his defeat of the Infidel. His victory over Don Sebastian's army was acclaimed generally as a triumph for Islam over Christianity, as soldiers from almost every European nation had come to Morocco to fight under the Portuguese banner. The first Muslim ambassadors to congratulate the new sovereign were the Algerians, and they were followed by others from Istanbul, from Gao – the capital of the Songhay Empire – and from Ngazargamu, capital of Bornu. All of the ambassadors were sent to congratulate Ahmad on the success of his triumphant *jihad*.

Ahmad was condescending and discourteous towards the African envoys, and actively hostile towards the Ottomans. He claimed that the gifts the Turks had brought him were paltry, complaining that he had been slighted and treated as a vassal. Their offering, he said, contrasted with the spectacular embassy sent by Philip II and the sumptuous gifts that came with it, which pleased him greatly and induced him to respond with great warmth.

The truth of the matter was that Ahmad had been keen from the outset to remove himself from the orbit of Ottoman suzerainty. The Ottoman sultan Selim I had conquered Egypt in 1517, and by virtue of his possession of the holy cities of Mecca and Medina had declared himself *amir al-mu'minin*, 'commander of the Faithful' (the caliphal title), and *khalifat rasul Allah*, 'the lieutenant of God's Messenger' (i.e. caliph). These titles declared the Ottoman caliphate's spiritual and political supremacy over the whole of the Muslim world, the *dar al-Islam*. In Morocco, because of Selim's claim to this title, the Sa'dian sultans prior to Ahmad ordered that the Ottoman caliph was to be named in the *khutba*, the Friday sermon, in explicit recognition of this supremacy. However, Ahmad al-Mansur ordered this practice to be abandoned, instructing that the Friday sermon should be preached in his name instead. He also decided to lead the Friday prayers personally, and soon declared himself caliph and *amir al-mu'minin*, a clear demonstration of his perception of himself as worthy of such honours, to be the *imam* of the Muslims and leader of the *jihad*.

There was no immediate Ottoman reaction to Ahmad's claim to the caliphate. Istanbul was busy with peace negotiations with Spain as well as the nadir of its war with Safavid Iran. But Ahmad's frosty reception of the Ottomans reveals that his rise to power led to a complete change in Morocco's relations with the Ottoman Empire, and his haughty attitude shows something of the extent of his personal ambitions.

Apart from these personal ambitions, the fact was that Morocco was geographically located between Habsburg Spain and Ottoman Turkey and thus occupied a crucial intermediate point between two major rivals for control of the Mediterranean. Ahmad al-Mansur was compelled perpetually to counterbalance the influence of Spain and the Ottomans without becoming openly hostile to or making a clear alliance with either power. Maintaining an equilibrium between, and thus independence from, both empires was the central strategy of Al-Mansur's diplomatic activity. The second thrust of his diplomacy was monitoring and mitigating the reactions of the countries of northern Europe which faced the consequences of his victory at Alcazar, above all the union of the crowns of Spain and Portugal in the person of Philip II. The third impetus of his diplomacy was a desire to participate in the conquest and colonization of the Americas. Al-Mansur understood well that the only way forward for his country was the Atlantic, and that a share in the New World would ensure that Morocco formed a part of the league of modern nations.

THE SPANISH REACTION TO ALCAZAR: THE CAPTIVE PRINCES

After the battle of Alcazar, Muley al-Shaykh (not to be confused with Ahmad al-Mansur's son, Muhammad al-Shaykh al-Ma'mun), the son of the dethroned sultan Muhammad al-Mutawakkil, who was supported by Portugal, took shelter with Muhammad's brother, Muley al-Nasr, in the Portuguese fortified town of Mazagan (on Morocco's Atlantic coast), along with the surviving remnants of the Portuguese army. Muley al-Shaykh, a boy of some fourteen or fifteen years of age, sailed to Lisbon with the Portuguese. After the death of Don Henrique (the aged cardinal who had inherited the Portuguese throne) in late 1580, Philip II succeeded in being named heir by the Portuguese court ahead of the other pretender, Don Antonio, Prior of Crato, who took refuge in England. As soon as he entered Lisbon, Philip II took charge of the two Moroccan princes, well aware of the negotiating power that holding them would represent for his future dealings with Morocco. During the next decade, the hostage princes would play an important role as pawns in international politics. By retaining the two exiled Moroccan princes in Spain, Philip II followed the example of the Ottoman sultan who had promoted Abd al-Malik, a refugee prince in Ottoman territory, against the latter's brother, Abdallah, the sultan of Morocco; the Turks would attempt to use the same policy with Muley Isma'il, Abd al-Malik's son, who was a permanent threat to his uncle Ahmad al-Mansur. All three princes – Muley Shaykh, Muley al-Nasr and Muley Isma'il – were potential rivals with the capacity to destabilize the domestic situation in Morocco.

In the beginning, Spain did not exploit the two captive princes in its negotiations with Morocco. In 1580, there was talk of joint

Spanish–Moroccan action against Algiers. In 1581, a twenty-year peace treaty between the two countries was signed that committed Spain to assisting Morocco against any Ottoman offensive. In exchange for this commitment, the Spaniards were promised control of the Atlantic port of Larache, which was also sought after by the Turks. This was a promise that Ahmad would periodically postpone or renegotiate, depending on how close the Turkish threat appeared to be. Larache, however, was important to Philip II, who planned to use it as a naval base for the defence of Spanish shipping routes to the West Indies.

During the early 1580s, Philip II strove to maintain friendly relations with Ahmad for fear that the Moroccan sultan might look to the Turks for aid. The abundant correspondence between Ahmad and the Spanish court is warm and courteous, though somewhat wary, throughout this period. In 1584, for example, Ahmad asked Philip respectfully to allow the Spanish artist Antonio López to continue his work on the decoration of the great al-Badi' palace that he was building in Marrakesh. Other letters discuss the purchase and sale of jewels, the liberation of captives, ransom payments for Portuguese noblemen, or attempts to protect the interests of the many Spanish merchants who traded in Morocco. Like England, Spain had an agent in Marrakesh who acted as a kind of consul, and who was responsible for trade affairs and the management of ransom payments for captives. This agent also reported to the Spanish court, carried out diplomatic missions or even espionage and provided the Spanish king and the Duke of Medinasidonia with an insider's view. These agents and traders from England and Spain produced an enormous amount of correspondence and other paperwork that constitutes a valuable source of information on the state of Morocco in the late sixteenth century.

ENGLAND AND THE CAUSE OF THE PORTUGUESE RESTORATION

The European ambassadors arrived in Morocco soon after the battle of Alcazar. In addition to the Spanish delegation sent by Philip II, envoys were sent from Portugal, Venice, Tuscany, France and England. Until the end of the sixteenth century, European diplomatic relations with Morocco revolved around support for the restorationist cause in Portugal: most nations supported another pretender to the throne, Don Antonio, Prior of Crato, who, it was hoped, would restore an autonomous Portugal. As we will see, this matter would become one of the primary bonds of friendship between Morocco and England. And this was not the only source of common interest: Ahmad al-Mansur was deeply intrigued by the English voyages of discovery, England's opening of new commercial routes and its emergence as Spain's primary rival, especially in the New World.

From late 1579, when it became clear that a union of the crowns of Portugal and Spain was about to transpire, some English political strategists began to publish communications that recommended alliances with both Morocco and Algeria as a means of increasing local pressure on Spain. These alliances were intended not only as a defensive measure against the growing power of Philip II, but also as a stage in a potential joint invasion of southern Spain. It was hoped, at any rate, that an alliance with Morocco would allow the English to establish a naval base in Mogador (the modern port of Al-Sawira/Essaouira) for the purpose of making attacks on the Spanish fleets en route to both West and East Indies. At the same time as English ships had a target in the coasts of Spain, English pirates ventured into the Mediterranean to attack what prey might appear, and used Moroccan ports as shelters.

English political interests in Morocco were also heightened by mutual economic and commercial ventures. The British struggle against Spain required an increase in the production of munitions, and hence an increased demand for saltpetre, an essential ingredient in gunpowder. Saltpetre, or potassium nitrate, was mined in Morocco and supplied to the English for decades. For his part, Ahmad al-Mansur aimed to build up his own fleet, an undertaking that called for timber, rigging, sails and other shipbuilding supplies, as well as arms, which only the English were prepared to sell to him.

THE BARBARY COMPANY

There was a marked increase in English trade with Morocco from the middle of the sixteenth century onwards. Most of the traders dealing with Morocco were based in London, and they included some of the most important merchants in the City. The main products they bought were Moroccan sugar and molasses, but also dates, almonds, wax, ivory and finely tanned goatskins known as Tafilalt, after the name of the region where they were produced. The English also imported raw materials from Morocco, such as the above-mentioned saltpetre, as well as copper.

English traders exported to Morocco various kinds of cloth and textiles. Many were used locally, while others were sold on to the 'Sudan' (meaning the lands south of the Sahara desert in the west of Africa, not the territories we now know as Sudan). The most common of these was the so-called 'sade blewes', a thin cloth dyed sky blue in colour and known as *burnatha* in Arabic. English traders succeeded in making this cloth so fashionable among the sultan's subjects that some sources claim the whole country was becoming tinged with blue. An English woollen textile called 'kersey' was also imported into Morocco. Nevertheless, the most important sector of English trade was undoubtedly that of arms and munitions. The English sold matchlocks, muskets, harquebuses, guns, sword blades, iron lances, chain-mail armour, gunpowder, bullets and cannonballs to Morocco. English traders also sold metals, such as tin, necessary for the soldering of artillery weapons.

The English trade with Morocco carried risks because of the consensus amongst Christian nations that weapons should not be sold to infidels. This consensus existed even before a Papal bull prohibited such trade explicitly, though it held sway only over the Catholic countries that recognized its authority. English ships carrying arms and munitions to Morocco were liable to be intercepted and their cargoes captured on the high seas by vessels from Catholic nations. Indeed, a number of Spanish army ships were specifically charged with patrolling the seas in an attempt to curb this controversial trade.

Numerous diplomatic complaints concerning the trade in arms were also made to Elizabeth I, not only by Spain and Portugal, but also by France. Conflicts also arose between English traders and other Europeans in Morocco who thought that the English were engaged in a contraband trade unfit for Christians, as well as competing unfairly.

The trade in contraband produced huge profits. The inherent political conflicts combined with the enormous profits gained from the Moroccan trade meant that an influential sector of London merchants did not want to see it monopolized, or potentially jeopardized, by a handful of individuals. This led to the creation of the Barbary Company in 1585 for a period of twelve years. The Barbary Company was founded on the model of similar corporations already functioning in England. The Levant Company, for example, was founded in 1581 to oversee the importation of pepper and other spices from an enormous trading zone that stretched from South-East Asia to the Middle East.

The Barbary Company was assigned the regulation and channelling of all commercial deals between Morocco and England. The Company had an agent based in Marrakesh who, on occasion, doubled as the representative of the Queen at the sultan's court. In fact, a number of traders from the Company performed diplomatic roles. Such was the case of Roger Bodenham, who in 1580 proposed the notion of a secret treaty between England and Morocco, and promoted himself as a possible negotiator of its terms. Several of the English traders who lived in Marrakesh, or who spent several months a year there, came to have close ties with Ahmad al-Mansur, who saw them as valuable sources of information. Jasper Thomson, a merchant living in Marrakesh, wrote to his brother Richard in July 1599 that when the sultan discovered that he had followed an expedition of the Ottoman sultan Selim to Hungary he asked him for a detailed account of the journey and questioned him about it for several days before instructing one of his secretaries to record an Arabic version of his account. When Thomson told Ahmad that the Habsburgs had laid siege to Buda and that the Turks had suffered great losses there, the sultan showed great joy: 'he hath sent for me sondry tymes since and has examined me uppon many particularities concerninge the Gran Siegnor and his proceedinges, for I see nothinge ys more pleasinge to the Kinge then to heare that the Turkes afaires proceeded not well'. It is clear from Thomson's remarks that Ahmad's loathing and fear of the Turks were even greater than his hatred for Spain at this time.

THE IBERIAN UNION

The union of the Portuguese and Spanish crowns under Philip II in 1580 produced both fear and wariness in the kingdoms of northern Europe and new alliances arose between them against Spanish hegemony. In 1585, the English signed the Nonsuch Treaty, known after the name of the English palace where it was signed, which committed Britain to aiding the Netherlands in its ongoing war with Spain. Elizabeth's alliance with the Dutch, which recognized the Netherlands as an independent nation, deeply shocked Philip II, for whom the territory was nothing more than a 'rebellious province'. Elizabeth I further distanced Philip II by recognizing Don Antonio, the candidate to the throne supported by the restorationist movement in Portugal, as the *de jure* king so as to allow trade with the Portuguese Empire 'usurped' by Philip II. The English also sheltered a number of leading Portuguese restorationists. With English assistance, these exiles tried to form an alliance with Ahmad that would help them recover the Portuguese throne.

The year 1585 also saw the start of the struggle between England and Spain for control of the oceans and sea trade routes. In April, Sir Richard Granville left England for Roanoke Island, where he founded the first (though short-lived) English colony in America, and in September Elizabeth I authorized Sir Francis Drake to intercept the Spanish silver fleets. Drake and his men sacked Vigo in northern Spain and sailed as far as Santo Domingo and Cartagena, which they also sacked. In 1587 he led an attack on Cadiz. The narrative of Drake's successful voyage was included in Richard Hakluyt's *Principal Navigations*, a collection of narratives of exploration, accounts of new worlds and lists of merchandise, assembled by its editor as an incentive for English voyages of discovery and trade.

Philip II signed a peace treaty with the Ottomans which held good for the Mediterranean, but confrontations with the Turks continued in the Indian Ocean – Spain now ruled over the Portuguese colonies there. English, Dutch and French adventurers and privateers intensified their harassment of Spanish ships in the Atlantic when Don Antonio began to grant letters of marque authorizing privateer attacks on Spanish shipping to virtually any ship-owner who requested them. The English navy and still more the English privateers became a permanent source of strain on trade and communications between Spain and its overseas provinces. All of these pressures helped Philip II to imagine that it was possible to bring England's naval power to an end, and preparations were made for the great Armada.

From his exile in England Don Antonio had since early 1586 sought support from the sultan of Morocco for his claim on the Portuguese throne. Ahmad corresponded with Don Antonio – and with Elizabeth I – on the subject of Don Antonio's ambitions. Ahmad agreed to discuss the matter in Marrakesh, without commitment. One of the participants in the negotiations was Henry Roberts, a Barbary Company employee. In 1588, Ahmad promised him authorization to return to London with a Moroccan ambassador in order to formalize the details of the pact with Don Antonio and Elizabeth I. The arrival of the two men was awaited anxiously in London, but Ahmad delayed their departure from Morocco until he knew the outcome of Philip II's attack on England.

News of the defeat of the Invincible Armada reached Marrakesh quickly and, upon hearing it, English, Dutch and French inhabitants of the city staged a display of great jubilation outside the home of the Spanish agent there, Diego Marín. Marín emerged from his home in an angry mood, swinging his sword and dagger, and killed several of those who insulted the name of Spain. The sultan ordered his immediate imprisonment, and he spent several years in jail in Marrakesh. Now Ahmad was free to give the go-ahead to negotiations with Don

Antonio and the English. Don Antonio sent his son, Don Cristobal, to Morocco as a guarantee for the funds Don Antonio promised to send Ahmad in exchange for his assistance in regaining the throne of Portugal. Don Cristobal became another captive prince who equalized the pressure exerted by Philip II through the Moroccan princes held in Spain.

The Moroccan ambassador, Marzuq Rais, travelled with Henry Roberts to London in January 1589. He was authorized to offer aid to the English in the form of men, money and foodstuffs, free access to Moroccan ports, Ahmad al-Mansur's personal intervention in the struggle against Spain, and a supply of water for the English fleet's next expedition to Portugal. In the meantime, the English fleet was preparing for its Portuguese expedition, under the command of the Earl of Essex; among the officers were Drake and Norris. The English hoped that Ahmad would provision the fleet in Morocco and would give them the assistance his ambassador had promised.

The ships sailed in 1589, heading first to La Coruña, which was duly sacked, and continuing on to Lisbon. The ambassador, Marzuq Rais, dressed as a Portuguese nobleman, was present throughout the expedition, sailing on the same ship as Don Antonio himself. The expedition disembarked near Lisbon, disastrously. The expected popular support for Don Antonio never materialized. In Lisbon, the English were rejected and were eventually forced to return to London with great losses in June of that year (1589).

The English blamed the failure on Ahmad, who had not kept his promise to provide material aid. However, behind the scenes, Philip II had engaged in a series of negotiations to undermine the Anglo-Moroccan alliance. His espionage service in Morocco had sent him copies of Ahmad's correspondence with Don Antonio and the English, so that he understood Ahmad's weaknesses and general reluctance to commit aid to the English. In Philip's own negotiations with Ahmad, he exploited the two captive Moroccan princes held in Andalusia, described in Spanish documents as *los infantes moros*, the Moorish princes. With great drama, the two princes were moved to Carmona (near Seville) in southern Spain in order to heighten

Ahmad's anxiety, the threat being that it would have been easy for them, with a modicum of Spanish assistance, to cross the Strait of Gibraltar to Morocco. Such a crossing would almost certainly have led to the outbreak of another civil war in Morocco. Ahmad's sensitivities to the threat of the *infantes moros* show how insecure he was concerning his own position and the loyalty of some of his subjects.

Probably in September 1589, Juan de Cárdenas, a Spanish exile who worked as a secretary to Walsingham, the queen's privy councillor, was sent to Marrakesh with instructions to agree the terms of a new pact between England and Morocco. This mission failed completely. Ahmad refused to meet the special envoy, to whom it was made known that the Moroccans were not prepared to hand over Don Antonio's captive son. Philip II and Ahmad depended entirely upon each other, and upon the assistance each might choose to give the rival prince he held hostage. But, when he saw the pressure that the English continued to exert on Ahmad, Philip II ordered the evacuation of Asila (the Portuguese port on the Moroccan Atlantic coast which had passed into Spanish hands) in order to ingratiate himself with the sultan. Philip also decided to renounce his claim to the port of Larache.

The situation was complicated further in June of 1590. Hassan Veneciano, the pasha of Algiers who had married Abd al-Malik's widow and had Muley Isma'il, Abd al-Malik's son, at his side, prepared a military intervention against Morocco, with Ottoman consent, in defence of Muley Isma'il's right to the throne. Faced with the danger of an Ottoman intervention in support of his nephew, Ahmad turned to Spain for assistance, offering to hand over Don Cristobal in exchange for military aid.

Meanwhile, the Ottomans staked a claim for Don Antonio's pretensions to the Portuguese throne through diplomatic contacts with England with the aim of an Anglo-Turkish alliance against Spain. Mathias Becudo, an envoy of Don Antonio who had lived at the court in Marrakesh since 1586, succeeded in becoming such a close personal friend of Ahmad al-Mansur that the Spanish ambassador wrote to his king to caution that Becudo was always at the sultan's side and always defended his interests. The thought-provoking correspondence between Becudo and Don Antonio reveals that Ahmad al-Mansur did not trust Elizabeth I's intention to put Don Antonio on the Portuguese throne, and Becudo did not recommend an English alliance with the Ottomans. According to Becudo, the Ottomans feared that Hassan Veneciano would declare the regency of Algiers independent, and wanted to avoid further conflicts in the Western Mediterranean.

In mid-1592, before the envoy from the Sublime Porte arrived in Marrakesh to claim Don Cristobal and take him to Istanbul, Ahmad decided to allow the Portuguese prince to sail for England. Three years later, in 1595, Don Antonio died, and his cause ceased to be a mechanism for the destabilization of Spain and the Iberian union. As for the two *infantes moros*: Muley al-Shaykh, Ahmad's nephew exiled in Spain, converted to Catholicism in 1593 and spent the rest of his life at the court in Madrid under the name of Don Felipe of Africa, Prince of Fez and Morocco. A short time later, after the death of Don Antonio, Philip II authorized Muley al-Nasr to cross the Strait of Gibraltar, without Spanish military or economic aid. However, he was not given permission to remain in the Spanish colony of Melilla for more than a few hours. Philip II warned Ahmad al-Mansur about the imminent arrival of the dethroned sultan, Muhammad's brother, justifying it by claiming that Muley al-Nasr and his large retinue had caused a number of serious disturbances in Carmona and had been found to be in contact with local Moriscos whom he had incited to rebellion. Despite the fact that Philip had provided no military aid to Muley al-Nasr, Ahmad was furious.

Muley al-Nasr sailed to Melilla and entered Moroccan territory with a small army of Renegades and Moriscos. Despite this incursion, Ahmad did not suspend diplomatic relations with Spain, although Spain's commercial agent in Morocco, Baltasar Polo, was imprisoned for several months until Muley al-Nasr was defeated. But, from then on, Ahmad's resentment of Philip II was permanent. And with cause: despite invading Morocco with a small force, Muley al-Nasr managed to take control of a wide area in the north of the country, which rose up in support, and even succeeded in conquering the city of Taza, now on the Moroccan border with Algeria. Muley al-Nasr was eventually defeated by Muley al-Shaykh, Ahmad's eldest son, governor of Fez and crown prince. But, alarmingly, Muley al-Shaykh gathered a powerful army around himself that he soon used to revolt against his father. This attack came as a terrible political and personal shock to Ahmad al-Mansur, who was deeply attached to his eldest son. In his letters to the pious Egyptian *'ulama* he often consulted for support and spiritual assistance, al-Bakri and al-Qarafi, Ahmad described this terrible blow and the threat it represented to his realm. The Egyptian *shaykhs* recommended the execution of Muley al-Shaykh, for Ahmad's own good and that of his realm, but the sultan chose not to follow their advice.

CADIZ AND AMERICA

The relationship between Elizabeth I and Ahmad al-Mansur had not ended. Don Antonio's sons, the Portuguese pretenders Don Cristobal and Don Manuel, went to the Dutch Republic, another of Spain's enemies, to ask for help. They asked the Dutch to make contact with Morocco on their behalf. The Dutch already had merchants in Morocco, and had close relations and treaties signed with England.

In July 1596 the Dutch Republic and England joined in an attack against the city of Cadiz in southern Spain. The expedition, led by Lord Howard, famously included Sir Walter Raleigh in the confederation. The confederates scattered the Spanish navy in the bay of Cadiz and, after bombarding the city from the bay, succeeded in taking control of it for a brief period. The attackers then sacked the city and set fire to it before leaving with booty. Raleigh played a major role in the raid of the Spanish galleons at Cadiz, where he was seriously injured. The English, in a gesture of goodwill towards Morocco, sent thirty-eight Moroccan captives, who had escaped from Spanish galleys during the fighting, back to their own country. The Dutch, also understanding the potential benefits of an alliance with Morocco and wishing to court the sultan's favour, sent him a leading citizen of Fez who had been held prisoner in Cadiz. They also informed the sultan that the Dutch intention had never been to leave Cadiz, but rather to request Moroccan aid to occupy it permanently and, once it was conquered, to hand the city over to Morocco, as an open door into the Peninsula through which to begin recovering formerly Islamic territory.

The Cadiz raid made a considerable impression on Ahmad al-Mansur, but it brought him closer to Elizabeth I than to the Dutch. The successful attack on Cadiz reignited the sultan's ambitious plan to invade and conquer southern Spain with the help of the English, an ambition that was no doubt nourished by the Moriscos in his inner circle. His intentions are made clear in one of the private letters he wrote to his scholarly advisers in Egypt, asking for their prayers. Now that Philip II had been defeated, he wrote, he had decided to undertake the conquest of Andalusia with the aim of creating conditions so that the true religion could be reborn there and the imperceptible remains of Islam revived. Ahmad wrote similar letters to scholars in the holy cities of Mecca and Medina.

In addition to seeking spiritual support and, thus, legitimacy, from Egypt and Arabia, after Philip II's death in 1598, Ahmad al-Mansur began to send envoys to England again. The first contact was initiated by the *qadi* Azzuz, who approached Jasper Thomson – the English merchant in Marrakesh – on the sultan's behalf. Through Azzuz, Ahmad tried to justify the lack of support given to the English during the Drake and Norris expedition, saying that the concurrent conquest of Sudan had left him short of men. Ahmad used the invasion of Sudan, as we will see, and the wealth and experience it brought him as proof that he was capable of undertaking conquests, and more than capable of performing even greater tasks. Azzuz told Thomson that, in the sultan's opinion, with another seven or eight thousand cavalrymen Cadiz would have been conquered and occupied permanently, and that Morocco could easily have supplied them. In response, Thomson refrained from offering an opinion, and instead suggested that the project should be the objective of a fresh Moroccan embassy to London. 'In the end,' wrote Thomson, 'his speech tended to this purpose, wither the Quene would be content to make such another army to land in some port in Spaine with 20 thowsand footemen, and with vessels to transport 20 thowsand horses and men from Barberie, and soe to joyne together in conquest of the contrye.'

THE MOROCCAN EMBASSY TO ENGLAND

A Moroccan embassy left for England early in the summer of 1600. The mission was meant to be confidential, and its true aims were unknown to almost everyone in Morocco. The entire mission was carried out with great deliberation and care. Officially, its aim was to purchase precious stones, and the Moroccans sailed first towards Aleppo so as not to arouse suspicion among the inevitable Spanish observers.

The embassy was headed by Sidi Abd al-Wahid al-Mansur Annuri, and seconded by Sidi al-Hajj Massa, later described as having 'great skill in all manner of pedreria [sic, 'precious stones'], as in dia-mondes, rubies and such lyke'. Sidi Abd al-Wahid 'speaketh a lytle Spanish, after the manner of the Moores', according to the merchant Jasper Thomson, who knew the real motives of the embassy because of his friendship with the Morisco interpreter Sidi Abdallah Dodar, a 'verie honest man' who travelled as official translator. Sidi Abdallah Dodar spoke both Spanish and Italian as a result of a spell spent as a Spanish soldier in Italy.

The Moroccan embassy landed at Dover in August, and in September Abd al-Wahid sent the queen a memorandum proposing an alliance with Ahmad against Spain. The sultan would supply troops, munitions, food and water supplies, and would allow the use of a Moroccan port, which he would equip with all that was necessary for the English navy; the port would be used as a shared base from which to sail for America and the West Indies. Bearing in mind, the memorandum stated, that the King of Spain's strength lay in the West and East Indies, a joint Anglo-Moroccan conquest of those territories was essential. If Spain were deprived of its sources

1600

ABDVLGVAHID.

LEGATVS REGIS BARBARIÆ
IN ANGLIAM.

ÆTATIS:42.

The Moorish Ambassador, Sidi Abd al-Wahid Annuri (The University of Birmingham Collections)

of wealth, the memorandum reasoned, it would be simple enough to weaken it.

It is clear that Ahmad al-Mansur was well-informed of the extent and geographical locations of Spanish and Portuguese colonies overseas, and what he hoped to accomplish was to incorporate some of them into his own empire. The possession of territories overseas would allow him to make alliances with other neighbouring Muslim countries, the sultan wrote, possibly referring to the Portuguese territories in the Strait of Hormuz, in Goa, India, or perhaps in East Africa. Ahmad was also aware, it seems, of the English quest for a North-West Passage through North America, a direct route to the East Indies.

Treaty arrangements would have to stipulate, Ahmad wrote, exactly how the conquered lands would be divided between Morocco and England. The sultan must have been thinking of the treaty of Tordesillas a century earlier (1494), when Portugal and Spain split the known map of the world between them. Ahmad alluded to the experience he had acquired in the conquest of Sudan (in the Arabic sense of the land to the south of the Sahara) and its incorporation in his empire. Given the proven capacity of his men for fighting and living in hot climes, he proposed that the Moroccans should be the ones left to colonize the newly conquered lands. This was another detail of the treaty that needed to be thrashed out, 'wether we shall take it in our chardg to inhabite it with our armie without yours in respect of the great heat of the clymat, where those of your countrie doo not fynde themselfes fitt to endure the extremitie of heat there, where our men endure it very well by reason that the heat hurtes them not'. The sultan's memorandum also included a request that an English ambassador be sent to Marrakesh to discuss the details of the operations and to agree upon a definitive version of the treaty.

As we have seen, Ahmad al-Mansur was well aware, even at the start of his reign, of Hispano-Portuguese activities in the Americas and their implications. Francis Drake, who circumnavigated the world between 1577 and 1580, returned home rich with plunder from Spanish settlements and ships. He stopped to restock his fleet in Mogador on the Moroccan Atlantic coast. Drake had come from, among other things, attacking the Peruvian port of Callao, and presenting a plan to his queen for conquering some of the American territories. The corsair ships that left Moroccan ports to attack vessels en route to the Indies brought back booty that was sold in the markets in Morocco, and thus American products were well-known there. Many of the Spanish Moriscos who fled Spain after the war of the Alpujarras escaped through Seville, the great port where ships returning from America would arrive. All of these factors contributed to Ahmad's understanding of overseas developments. But above all, as we have seen, Ahmad was in contact with English merchants, whom he enjoyed quizzing about all sorts of subjects. As a result, he shared the English perception of America both as a source of great wealth and as a possible passage to the eastern Muslim lands that would avoid the Ottoman lands. Also, having American colonies was a sign of immense political power. Ahmad's interests in acquiring all kind of navigational and astrological devices in England become crystal-clear.

The Moroccan ambassadors in London

The Moroccan envoys arrived in London in September 1600, escorted by the most important of the English merchants who traded in Morocco. They were lodged close to the Royal Exchange, at the home of Alderman Ratcliffe, and were received with frosty suspicion. The queen, who was at Nonsuch, conceded an audience to them on 30 September and another some weeks later at Oatelands. On 27 November – the anniversary of Elizabeth's coronation – they witnessed the great ceremony of celebration at Whitehall, where they were accorded places of honour.

The hospitality and lodging provided for the visitors were problematic: the Moroccans insisted on following their own dietary rules and on slaughtering poultry or mutton themselves for meat; they refused to give alms to the poor, allegedly because the poor were Christian and therefore undeserving of their charity. Their religious observance seems to have reminded their English hosts of Catholic practices, as it was observed that 'they use beades and pray to saints'. Most of the enmity and suspicion that was directed towards them was provoked by the London merchants, who claimed that the mission to establish a treaty with England was a pretext, and that the ambassadors had come, in reality, for commercial espionage.

During the six months they spent in London they were alleged to have been diligent and ingenious in their gathering of information about prices, weights, measures and the kinds of commodities sent to London or exported from it. They purchased different varieties of weights and measures, and kept several samples of commodities. They also showed a great interest in acquiring information about the price of sugar exported to Europe, and the profits made on it by merchants involved in its trade. Above all, they were seen to want to acquire maps of the new American territories, and information on the much sought-after North-West Passage which, it was thought, would allow transit to the East. 'It was generally judged, by their demeanors, that they were rather espials [sic] than honorable ambassadors,' as one of the merchants wrote. Why did the Moroccan ambassadors arouse so much suspicion?

The answer to this question lies in the fact that they had arrived in England at a particularly significant and sensitive moment in commercial terms. In September 1599, the cream of London's merchant class assembled at Founders Hall. Over a hundred traders, from Lord Mayor Soame and the leading aldermen to prosperous drapers and grocers, had convened a few weeks earlier to form a joint stock company. They chose directors and a treasurer, and drafted a petition to the queen 'for the honour of our native country and for the advancement of trade . . . to set forth a voyage this present year to the East Indies'. Thus was the East India Company born, a company that, as it grew, played a vital role in forging the British Empire.

Until now, England had failed to settle permanent colonies in the Americas. English adventurers had not succeeded in breaking into the Caribbean slave trade, nor had they discovered the famous North-West Passage, and they had failed to establish commercial endeavours in the East Indies through the long sea route around the Cape of Good Hope. The Dutch, on the other hand, had already gained access to the eastern trade. Dutch ships with rich cargoes arrived in Amsterdam from Java that same year of 1599. The English were fully cognizant of Dutch attempts to penetrate the Moroccan market and establish an alliance with Sultan Ahmad. At the time of the Moroccan embassy to London, the first East India Company expedition to sail around the Cape of Good Hope was already being outfitted, and was to set out in 1601. It is not surprising, then, that the English merchants felt uncomfortable about the enquiries made by the Moroccan ambassadors. To make matters worse, Sidi Abdallah Dodar, the interpreter, died unexpectedly: according to the rumour spread by some traders, he was poisoned by order of his own ambassador because of the friendship he had struck up with several English merchants. The mission therefore came to an abrupt end. The return to Morocco was organized swiftly and the Moroccans, against their wishes, were placed on a ship bound directly for Morocco. The Moroccans feared they might be intercepted or attacked by a Spanish vessel, and argued for a return voyage, again, via Aleppo.

THE SULTAN'S MEMORANDUM

The sultan's memorandum caused scepticism and a lack of confidence among the English, despite the ambassadors' best efforts to extol the Moroccan achievements in the conquest of Sudan. Robert Cecil, the queen's minister who studied the proposal, made the prudent recommendation to encourage what appeared to be goodwill on the part of the Moroccans and to try to take advantage of it. The sultan was informed that the idea of conquering Spanish territories in the Indies was more attractive and seemed more advisable than making attacks directly on the Iberian Peninsula. And Elizabeth (in accordance with al-Mansur's wishes) sent Henry Prannell, a merchant with connections in Morocco, to Marrakesh to negotiate with the sultan. The sultan's initial response was to request that he be sent an ambassador of a higher rank, but he eventually agreed to receive Prannell. Through the merchant, Elizabeth reiterated her refusal to take part in any project that involved attacking Spain directly, arguing that such attacks would benefit neither Morocco nor England.

On the other hand, she did maintain an interest in forging an alliance to intensify the campaigns of interception of Spanish ships coming and going to the Indies. The Queen also requested Ahmad's assistance in promoting further discoveries overseas, asking the sultan for an initial sum of £100,000 to help her rebuild and improve her navy.

This plan was accepted by the sultan, who continued to show great interest in overseas adventures, although he replied that he was reluctant to advance the funds to her before a treaty was signed. Ahmad claimed to have the monies prepared, but for their delivery, he required an adequate English embassy and a fully equipped warship to come and take charge of them. The treaty was never finalized, although Ahmad endeavoured to bring it to fruition in the last years of his life. He died in August 1603, just a few months after the queen of England.

AHMAD AND EL DORADO

Ahmad's familiarity with European ventures into American territory probably included knowledge of Sir Walter Raleigh's voyage of 1595–6. In 1595, Raleigh sailed to Guyana in South America (present-day Venezuela), with the intention of discovering new lands and riches for his queen, and of conquering the legendary kingdom of El Dorado for her.

Raleigh's account of the Guyana expedition, *Discovery of Guiana (The discoverie of the large, rich and bewtiful empire of Guiana, with a relation of the great and golden citie of Manoa (which the Spaniards call El Dorado))*, was published almost as soon as he returned to England, and translated into several languages. It circulated rapidly throughout Europe in multiple printed forms and editions, becoming one of the most popular travel accounts of the age of exploration. It was also a call to arms for those who would challenge Spain's hegemony in America. For the enemies of Spain, Guyana was the key to Spanish America. Centrally located between Mexico and the Caribbean to the north and Peru to the west and Brazil to the east, it was a pivotal piece of land and, as such, figured in many colonial initiatives of the late sixteenth century. Guyana, it was thought, might turn out to be the next Peru, a 'magazine of all rich mettels', as Raleigh himself put it, a new realm of prodigious wealth. To the enemies of Spain, Guyana was the key that unlocked Spain's empire.

Remarks in his letters and comments to traders indicate that Ahmad al-Mansur was familiar with the expedition and with Raleigh's account of it. It is unlikely that he would have read the book itself, but he probably knew about it through his contact with English and Dutch merchants, corsairs and captives. One such contact could have been Edmund Darcy, an Irishman of noble origin who had been a volunteer on Raleigh's voyage to Guyana and was later captured at Salé and sent as a gift to the court of Marrakesh. Ahmad clearly hoped for a share in the attack on the Spanish colonies in the Americas. In the end, however, it was the Dutch who managed to conquer and briefly hold the Brazilian region of Pernambuco, where they established their own sugar industry. The Brazilian sugar industry was to be the ruin of Moroccan sugar and, in many ways, of Morocco.

6

THE CONQUEST OF
WESTERN SUDAN

In search of another El Dorado – indeed the source of gold itself – Ahmad al-Mansur sent an armed force to conquer the Songhay kingdom of Gao and Timbuktu in 1591. The army comprised approximately five thousand soldiers, mainly Moriscos and Renegades, armed with matchlocks and harquebuses and a large convoy of cannons and heavy artillery. Ahmad's army crossed the Sahara, marching, astonishingly, across more than 2000 kilometres of desert terrain to reach the city of Gao or Kaghu (in present-day Mali), where it succeeded in bringing down the reigning Muslim sovereigns. The army was led by the renegade or Morisco Pasha Jawdar (confusingly, Moriscos who returned to Islam were routinely described as Renegades in European documents), who was born in a town in the province of Almería, in the old kingdom of Granada. In this Moroccan army, the orders were given in Spanish, with the result that Sudanese chronicles of the expedition contain Arabic transcriptions of phrases like 'Corten le la cabeza' ('Cut off his head'). The conquest of the Songhay kingdom, like so many others in that century, was a thoroughly brutal episode. One might compare it to Lope de Aguirre's ruthless expedition along the Amazon river in 1560. Its benefits for Morocco were dubious and the conquered territories did not stay in Moroccan hands for long. Nonetheless, it allowed Ahmad al-Mansur to add 'King of Guinea' to his titles.

Jawdar's march across the desert and his conquest of Gao and Timbuktu have almost been forgotten today. In 1599, after his return to Morocco, the conquered territories fell into chaos and their importance to Morocco was marginalized. However, there remains in Mali to this day a small sector of the population whose members claim descent from Jawdar's Morisco army. They refer to themselves as the 'Arma', the Spanish word for 'weapon'. They constituted a dominant military aristocracy in the region of the Niger Bend for several centuries, but are now a rather small and disenfranchised group. Within the complex understanding of the nuances of skin tones in Malian culture, the Arma classify themselves as 'white', although their colouring is no different from that of the rest of the local population.

SUDANESE GOLD

Tales had long been told of the vast and fabulous wealth to be found in the African kingdoms of the Western Sudan. Somewhere in Mali, Ghana or Songhay, those territories comprising the area south of the Sahara that Arabic chronicles called *bilad al-sudan* ('the land of the blacks'), there was believed to be a city of gold or brass equivalent to one mentioned in the Qur'an. The legend of the City of Gold was reinforced by traders who travelled along the caravan routes that had traversed the Sahara since the medieval period to carry the famous gold dust (*al-tibr*) northward. The Sudanese paid in *al-tibr* for salt and manufactured products, such as textiles. Travellers' tales helped to create fabulous rumours such as the one that claimed that the mosques of Timbuktu were built with walls of gold. Other Muslim travellers such as Ibn Battuta or Leo Africanus insisted that what was worth its weight in gold was not the golden or reddish adobe dust that covered Sudanese buildings, but the manuscripts in this region renowned for its devotion to Islamic intellectual study and writings. The dominant castes of the Sudan had been Muslim since the eleventh century, and by the sixteenth Timbuktu had become a rich centre of Islamic piety and scholarship.

THE CONQUEST OF WESTERN SUDAN **99**

But the Sudan's reputation as an El Dorado was not without cause. In 1325, an emperor of Mali, the Mandinga Mansa Musa, made a pilgrimage to Mecca with a large retinue of followers. He brought large quantities of gold with him that had been accumulated over several years from the mountains in northern Ghana. Mansa Musa's pilgrimage made such a great impression along the way that the well-known Mallorcan Jewish cartographer, Abraham Cresques, represented Mali in his 1375 map with a figure of Mansa Musa seated on a golden throne, with a golden sceptre and crown and holding a large gold nugget in his right hand. Cresques's perceptions of the gold of Mali came through Jewish traders who were active on the trans-Saharan trade routes.

Mansa Musa, incidentally, had sent Mali's first embassy to the sultan of Morocco, the Marinid Abu 'l-Hasan, in 1338. Some years later, when the sultan died and was succeeded by his son Abu 'Inan, Sudanese ambassadors travelled to Morocco, this time taking a giraffe with them as a gift for the new sovereign. The giraffe caused a sensation in Morocco. Nevertheless, official political relations between Sudan and Morocco did not flourish and these two diplomatic missions appear to be the only ones recorded. There was, however, constant contact between Moroccan and 'Sudanese' scholars, especially during their journeys to the Middle East.

Successive pilgrimages to Mecca by Sudanese sovereigns had a similar impact. Descriptions of their processions through Cairo are found in a number of different chronicles. For example, Askiya Muhammad (founder of the Askiya dynasty in 1493) apparently passed through Cairo in 1496. Accompanied by the chiefs of all the tribes of his kingdom, five hundred men on horseback and a thousand men on foot, he brought eighty camels laden with gold. Askiya Muhammad took advantage of his journey to Cairo to request recognition from the resident Abbasid caliph for his authority over the entire Songhay territory, from the land of Kunta to the Atlantic, including all the lands of the Niger river, and from Bendoukou to the salt mine of Teghazza in the middle of the Sahara desert.

According to Leo Africanus, Teghazza was a salt quarry from which salt was extracted like marble, in rectangular blocks that were loaded on to camels. The Teghazza mine was fundamental to the health of inhabitants of the Saharan regions, both human and bovine, and constituted a major source of wealth for Sudanese sovereigns. Control of the salt mines had been a bone of contention between Morocco and Songhay throughout the sixteenth century.

THE SAHARA

The Moroccan Sahara begins at the river Wadi Dra'a. The river descends from the summits of the High Atlas through the foothills of the Atlas mountain range, until it meets a high plateau that diverts it westward, where it eventually flows into the Atlantic. From the high plateau of the Dra'a, it is a march of five or six days across a terrain known as *hammada* (rocky desert) before one reaches the Erg Iguidi, where the sand desert begins. The terrain is composed of high dunes with corridors running between them. The desert of sand stretches as far as Taodeni, where some salt marshes lie, and continuing on from that point there is an even harsher desert terrain, where the distance between wells for water can reach more than 80 kilometres.

This unforgiving terrain was traversed regularly by camel caravans trading in salt, ivory, slaves and gold going up to the Moroccan Dra'a and to the city of Sijilmassa in the Tafilalt, a little further east, on the present-day border with Algeria. The caravans also carried ostrich feathers and indigo and took textiles, salt and various manufactured products to the south. The trade routes with 'Sudan' had always been of great economic importance to Morocco, and became even more so as Morocco's access and egress through its ports were cut off by the Spanish, Portuguese and Ottomans. Morocco's mistake, however, was to believe the legend that huge amounts of gold were to be found in Sudan, and that the apparently inexhaustible source would likewise confer boundless power on the sovereign who controlled it, making it a second Peru.

Long before Jawdar's conquest, in 1581, Ahmad al-Mansur sent large numbers of soldiers to take control of the clusters of oases in the Tuwat and Tigurarin regions, way-stations for the caravans crossing the Sahara. The occupation of these oases required Ahmad's soldiers to make a long march through the desert to the south and east of the Tafilalt, and was a test of their ability to overcome the difficulties of advancing in such terrain. In time, it became an expedition that would move the Moroccans closer to the border with Sudan.

According to the later explanations of his chroniclers, Ahmad planned to conquer Sudan from the time of that exercise in 1581. Whether or not this was true, another incentive arrived in Fez in January 1589. An embassy from the kingdom of Bornu, another Sudanese kingdom, situated to the east of Songhay territory, came seeking military aid. The King of Bornu held sway over the Fezzan region, south of present-day Libya, which meant that he controlled access to the routes of the caravans travelling east to Tripoli, Tunis and Cairo. From the 1550s onwards, the Ottomans began to travel as far as the Fezzan region, and the Bornu king Mai Idris Aloma (1564–96) established diplomatic relations with them. Although he maintained an embassy in Murat III's Istanbul for four years, Idris Aloma was largely unsuccessful in his attempts to procure mercenaries, firearms and access to the latest military technology from the Ottomans. He turned to Morocco with the same intentions, arguing that he needed such arms to conduct *jihad* against his pagan neighbours. But Bornu contacts with the Ottomans and their influence in this nearby African kingdom were not welcomed by Ahmad al-Mansur.

According to Ahmad al-Mansur's chroniclers, all the stops were pulled to impress the Bornu ambassadors with the Moroccan sultan's grandeur: they were granted an audience 'calculated to display his power' and his 'prophetic illumination'. Ahmad also sent Idris Aloma gifts, which included a number of 'prophetic garments'. However, he considered the use of arms and the *jihad* as prerogatives unique to the *imam* or caliph of the Muslims, and in Ahmad's view these titles belonged to him alone. By virtue of his prophetic lineage he was entrusted by God with leadership of the whole Islamic community (the *umma*) and with the earth's heritage, the Prophecy and the Message (we will return to the subject of these prophetic claims in due course). Thus Mai Idris Aloma was asked to recognize Ahmad al-Mansur's caliphal rights and to wage *jihad* against the Infidels in Ahmad's name rather than his own.

Ahmad employed a similar strategy in his dealings with the sovereigns of the Songhay Empire. He began by sending envoys who urged the Muslim princes of the Sudan to recognize his authority. Then, in 1588, he wrote to the Askiya Ishaq requesting a *mithqal* of gold for every load of salt extracted from the Teghazza mine. Ahmad made it known that this tax would finance armies of Islam which would be able to fight the Infidels and retake Andalusia. Before writing to Askiya Ishaq, Ahmad consulted the *'ulama* of his kingdom and his most skilled jurisconsults, who assured him that no mine could be exploited without the authorization of the *imam* of the Muslims. The letter to the Sudanese sovereign was drafted by the *mufti* of Marrakesh, one of the leading jurists of Morocco. However, Askiya Ishaq refused to pay the tax on his mines, or to recognize the Sultan of Morocco as his caliph.

When he received Askiya Ishaq's refusal, Ahmad al-Mansur gathered the *'ulama* and his courtiers together, and revealed that he had decided to attack the Sudan. This decision, he told them, was motivated by his desire to unite all the forces of Islam under a single command – his own – and to recover the territories Islam had lost. A land as wealthy as Sudan would be able to finance and strengthen the army of the Muslims. Moreover, Ahmad said, Askiya Ishaq could not aspire to the title of '*Imam* of the Muslims' because he was not from the lineage of the Quraysh, the tribe of the Prophet.

Upon hearing this explanation, the *'ulama* fell silent until, forced to speak, they pointed out the difficulties of such a journey, as well as the illegality of attacking a Muslim and Sunni country that had not committed a single act of aggression against Morocco. They also explained that no sultan from any previous known dynasty had ever considered such an undertaking, and, thus, that there was no precedent that might legitimize such an expedition. Ahmad replied that Andalusia had been shut off to the armies of Islam, and that Algiers was under Turkish control: an attack on Sudan was the only possible way to augment his wealth and find the necessary manpower to advance on these fronts. Furthermore, he argued, the Sudanese still fought with lances, arrows and swords and could be defeated easily by the sultan's well-armed artillerymen. Eventually, the Sultan overcame the *'ulama*'s resistance to his proposal.

This episode is highly significant even if it was related summarily by the chroniclers. On the one hand, it shows that Ahmad needed the support of the *'ulama* in order to be able to legitimize his actions to his subjects. On the other, it also reveals the limitations of the *'ulama*'s capacity to influence the sultan's decisions – their role seems to have consisted largely of sanctioning decisions that had already been taken. At the same time, it is also important to note that the reason for invading Sudan cited most often by the sultan was the acquisition of gold that would fund the reconquest of Andalusia. This idea would no doubt have been attractive to the Andalusians among the sultan's troops and may even have originated with them, as was suggested by several foreign agents in Morocco at the time.

THE EXPEDITION

The Sudan expedition left Marrakesh in October 1590, after several months of preparation. The departure was marked with great pomp and ceremony. Standards and banners were raised over battalions in perfect formation and it was said that 'the victory of God hung over them like a protective cloud'. Accounts in some detail survive of the preparations made for the expedition, noting what the soldiers took with them, and how they progressed. One of these accounts, an eye-witness report written in 1591 by an anonymous Spanish agent or merchant living in Marrakesh, is especially relevant. The Arabic sources from Morocco and Sudan reflect more of an interest in the happenings of the war and the booty that was acquired, as does the correspondence of a number of English traders in Morocco.

Ahmad carefully assembled a small but experienced army to carry out the raid on Sudan. It comprised two thousand harquebusiers divided evenly between Renegades and Moriscos from the kingdom of Granada, five hundred *espais* or mounted harquebusiers – almost all of them also Moriscos and Renegades – and fifteen hundred lancers recruited from the Arab tribes. The army was accompanied by a convoy carrying large amounts of army biscuit, gunpowder, light and heavy cannons of the type used to fire stone cannonballs in assaults on cities, a considerable quantity of wheat and barley for the animals, and, as the main sustenance for the men, dates crushed into a paste. All of this material was transported by more than ten thousand camels, which also carried munitions, clothing and tents. The soldiers also took ropes, picks, spades, burlap, resin and tar, clear signs that the army was prepared to lay siege to walled cities like those found in Morocco, though not found in Mali. The convoy was completed by a number of camel drivers, sappers, surgeons and other medical staff.

The longest stage of the march through the desert without fresh water was to last for twelve days, but there were also several three- and six-day stages, and, in readiness, the army carried water in full ox-skins. Each camel carried two such water 'tanks'. The water was for the use of the men and the horses, as the camels could go without water for up to a fortnight. In the desert, the army navigated with guides and compasses as if they were at sea, because of the lack of paths or other distinguishing features in the barren landscape.

The exhausting journey lasted thirty-five days. Many of the soldiers and animals died of hunger, sunstroke or dehydration before the army reached the river Niger close to Timbuktu. The survivors were so unwell and incapable of fighting that what was left of the army avoided the city altogether, and headed slowly eastward along the wooded left bank of the Niger towards Gao. Gao was Askiya Ishaq's capital and the base of his organized resistance to the invaders. Askiya Ishaq had gathered a sizeable army of men equipped with bows and arrows, plus a number of mounted soldiers armed with short lances or javelins. His army also had a large number of oxen, with which he planned to form a sort of mobile wall that would allow them to come close enough to the Moroccans to engage in hand-to-hand fighting whilst protecting themselves from projectiles fired by the Moroccan forces – they hoped these would bounce off the bodies of the oxen.

The encounter between the two armies took place in Tondibi, three marching stages from Gao, on 13 February 1591. The firearms of the Moroccans proved indomitable, despite the heroic resistance of the Songhay army. During the battle, the terrified oxen did no more than sow chaos and confusion as they backed off and charged their own army. The Sudanese had an elite corps of some eight thousand men, each of whom wore a gold armband. This corps chose to fight by placing a shield on the ground upon which each man knelt, tying his foot to his thigh. From such a position the soldiers fired their arrows and also showed their intention never to retreat. The example of this corps is said to have inspired the rest of the army to fight with greater courage and tenacity. However, the artillery fire of the invaders dispersed or killed so many of the Songhay infantrymen that in the end only the elite corps remained, its members fixed in their kneeling posture. As the Moroccans approached to fight them at close quarters, attacking them with sabres and tearing off their gold armbands, the immobile Sudanese warriors are reported to have said over and over to no avail: 'We are Muslims, we are your brothers in religion.'

Gao was evacuated amid great panic and many people were drowned in the river in the resulting mayhem. Askiya Ishaq, his family and entourage took refuge with the remains of his army on the right bank of the Niger. The victorious Jawdar entered Gao, but was hugely disappointed by what he saw: nothing but a hamlet of adobe houses. There was no gold, and the Askiya's palace was so primitive that it resembled the home of the head of the palace stables in Marrakesh. Jawdar then made an attempt to cross the mighty Niger by placing wooden rafts on the oxen water-skins, pumped full of air, but failed.

Askiya Ishaq, from his place of refuge, made a hasty offer of peace to Jawdar, promising to recognize Ahmad al-Mansur's suzerainty, to present him with 100,000 pieces of gold and a thousand slaves and to grant him a monopoly on the Sudanese salt trade. In exchange, he requested the immediate withdrawal of Moroccan troops. Jawdar sent a messenger to Ahmad with an account of this proposal, together with his own assessment that the Sudan was not worth occupying and that Askiya Ishaq's offer was a good one. Jawdar's message was accompanied by a gift of two hundred slaves and 10,000 *mithqals* of gold. Meanwhile, in Sudan, Jawdar's army was decimated by malaria and other local diseases, forcing him to move into Timbuktu while he waited for further instructions from Ahmad. He and his troops entered Timbuktu peacefully in April 1591. Ahmad received Jawdar's letter and gifts at about the same time.

The news from Jawdar enraged the Moroccan sultan. In Ahmad's view, Jawdar had been too quick to accept Askiya Ishaq's proposals, which the sultan deemed worthless without the sending of princes or other members of the ruler's family to guarantee the deal. Ahmad is said to have written in his own hand on the verso of the letter to Jawdar written by his secretary, the following remarks:

> Would you offer me money? What God has given me is better than what he has given you, though you rejoice in your gift. Return to them. We shall come to them with armies they have no power against and we shall expel them from their lands in a state of humiliation and abasement.

This text from the Qur'an (27: 36–37) is Solomon's response to the Queen of Sheba's offer of a gift in lieu of submitting to him. It is a fascinating example of Ahmad's rhetorical choices, quotations from the Qur'an or Traditions that integrated him with a glorious past and made him equal, in this case, to no less a figure than Solomon himself.

Solomon (or Sulayman), the biblical king, is a prominent personality in Islamic legend, endowed with esoteric knowledge and powers of magic and revelation. He was considered a symbolically important figure in the Qadiriyya Sufi brotherhood. In the Qur'an, Sulayman enjoys the distinction of being a divine messenger and a prototype of Muhammad. It will be seen, in the next chapter, how this quotation was part of an integrated effort towards legitimization of the sultan's actions.

Ahmad was irritated that Jawdar left Gao without building a fort there and leaving an occupying force in charge of the city. From the start, clearly, Ahmad's aim was to consolidate his conquest and transform Western Sudan into a province of Morocco. He removed Jawdar summarily from his post and replaced him with another renegade army general, the pasha Mahmud Zarqun, who, like Jawdar, had been brought up in the sultan's palace from an early age and had formed part of the sultan's personal guard. Mahmud Zarqun left Marrakesh with a group of forty men at the end of June, the most difficult time of the year to undertake a crossing of the Sahara. Mahmud Zarqun's orders included instructions to travel by night to avoid the worst of the heat. His mission was to replace Jawdar as governor of Sudan, continue the journeys of discovery and conquest and consolidate Moroccan power in Gao. He arrived eventually to Timbuktu in the middle of August. Jawdar offered no resistance to his dismissal, but stayed in Sudan to collaborate with Mahmud Zarqun. Mahmud Zarqun, however, had to deal with the revolt of the Sudanese *ulama*, who had refused to accept the authority of the Moroccan sultan. It was in the context of this predicament that Mahmud Zarqun sent the well-known Sudanese jurist Ahmad Baba al-Tumbukti to Marrakesh in chains, to the consternation of his Moroccan colleagues.

Ahmad al-Mansur seems to have caught the spirit of the Age of Discovery. He wanted his men to continue to sail down the river Niger in search of the source of *tibr* gold. A second expedition left Marrakesh in November under the command of Mansur Abd al-Rahman, a renegade of Spanish origin known by the diminutive 'Mansorico'. Mansorico travelled with five thousand riflemen – Moriscos, Renegades and Arabs from the tribes of the Sus – under instructions to supply Zarqun with reinforcements and then continue towards Guinea in the south.

For this mission, the sultan ordered a number of brigantines to be built in the Dra'a that could be packed up as separate components, each of the timbers marked with indications for later reassembly. The timbers were transported by camels through the Sahara: ships on camels carried through the ocean of the Sahara. Thus the Niger ceased to be an obstacle to further exploration, and Mahmud Zarqun was able to fulfil his mission by sailing down as far south as the gold-producing regions.

In August 1594, Lawrence Madoc, an English merchant in Marrakesh, wrote to his colleague Anthony Dassel in London, reporting on the arrival in the city of the chief of the 'Andalouzes, home from Gago . . . with thirty mules laden with gold. I saw the same come into the Alcasava with mine owne eies.' Mahmud Zarqun also brought back three sons of the King of Gao as guarantors, a new group of captive princes. In another letter a month later, Madoc wrote of the huge treasures Zarqun was said to have gathered in his expedition 'downe toward the sea coast': 'This King of Morocco is like to be the greatest prince in the world for money, if he keepe this countrey.' Ahmad al-Mansur's official court chronicler wrote that the gift sent by Mahmud Zarqun to his sovereign came to twelve hundred slaves (both male and female), forty cargoes of gold dust, four of solid gold and numerous cargoes of ebony, musk and civet, as well as a series of rare and expensive objects.

According to the Arab chroniclers, the conquest of Sudan provided Ahmad al-Mansur with so much gold that he was able to pay his civil servants and army in pure gold dinars. Mahmud Zarqun's exploits in the Sudan were celebrated for three days and nights on the streets of Marrakesh and at court. Official poets composed poems for the occasion that foreign ambassadors and observers were instructed to come and hear.

Jawdar remained in the Sudan until 1599. In September of that year, Jasper Thomson wrote to his brother Richard informing him of Jawdar's return to Marrakesh. Jawdar continued to serve his sultan loyally, and, after Ahmad's death, also served his son, Muley Zidan. Thomson described this faithful servant as a 'nobleman from Gago' who had been sent ten years earlier to conquer the Sudan. Thomson remarked also, in passing, that so many men from Morocco had lost their lives:

> He brought with him thirty camels laden with tyber which is unrefined gold (yet the difference is but six shillings in an once weight between it and duccattes) also great store of pepper, unicornes hornes and a certaine kind of wood for diyers [the corn plant, used for trading purposes in Morocco] to some 120 camel loads; all which he presented to the King with 50 horses and great quantity of eanuches, duarfes and weomen and men slaves besides 15 virgins, the Kings daughters of Gago which he send to be the Kings concubines.

Thomson remarked further: 'Yow must note all these be of the cole black heyre, for that contry yeldeth noe other.'

Eunuchs, dwarves, black slaves and exotic animals: the singular and the monstrous were the privileged material of expeditions of conquest and discovery throughout the sixteenth century. Monstrous beings were associated with the prodigious, connecting the natural world with the supernatural one, as Solomon himself had done. They were perceived as signs of divinity that could be interpreted prophetically. Such signs were to contribute to the dazzling and blinding display of power sought after by Ahmad's court at Marrakesh, and to the symbolic connection with the supernatural world, as we will see. Expeditions of discovery and conquest were steps in the achievement of a universal monarchy.

But, though the surface was brilliant, the Sudan expedition was always more about appearances than profits. The Sudan was not Peru. Morocco never succeeded in organizing or consolidating its base south of the Sahara. Governors of the Sudan came and went, spending their brief periods in office pillaging and looting for their own benefit. Only a fraction of the gold ever reached the sultan in Marrakesh, however spectacular the treasures appeared and however much they were lauded by court chroniclers and poets. The Sudan enterprise resulted in a huge loss of men, spent on an effort to hold on to a territory that was too distant, and which failed to provide the expected riches. Ahmad lost or diverted his best troops in the

Sudanese adventure at a time when, as we will see, they would have been much more useful to him at home. The prestige in the eyes of Northern European allies that Ahmad expected to realize by his conquest never materialized. And this was despite the best efforts of his ambassadors in England, who did not hesitate to exaggerate the significance of the Sudan mission: a memorandum by Abd al-Wahid preserved at the Public Record Office in London describes the vast kingdom of Guinea by the river Niger that had been won by his sultan, a kingdom whose perimeter could be marched around in ninety days, a region where eighty-six thousand towns and cities had been conquered , where occupying forces had been left to fortify the place under Ahmad's rule, because Moroccans were perfectly capable of enduring the heat of the land. This conquest, these experiences and qualities were presented as proof that Moroccans were fit to undertake other ventures in the Indies.

At home, moreover, the conquest created a problem of legitimacy for Ahmad that he tried to gloss over with a series of propaganda campaigns and the deployment of various ideological arguments. The use of these arguments, by means of which he tried to assume a quasi-sacred status, reveal something of his conflicts with the *'ulama* class, and also the weakness of his legitimate rule in the eyes of his own subjects. Ahmad financed a group of court secretaries, poets and official chroniclers who devoted a great many pages to the fine deeds and lavish feasts of their sultan, as well as constructing and spreading a legitimizing propaganda that sacralized the sovereign and endowed him with what are clear messianic characteristics.

7

THE CONSTRUCTION OF AN
IMPERIAL IDEOLOGY

The domestic problems to which Ahmad al-Mansur sometimes alluded in order to justify his failures to meet promises to various foreign nations were serious indeed, and he had to devote much of his energy to solving them. These domestic problems included uprisings of tribal confederations, claims to the caliphate from different candidates within his own family, and popular discontent with the heavy tax burden imposed by his regime.

At the beginning of his reign, al-Mansur introduced a series of far-reaching fiscal and economic measures designed to strengthen his country's economic condition, as well as its international standing, as mentioned already. He also undertook important reforms of the armed forces and administration. Among his economic measures were a revaluation of the currency and the introduction of restrictions on the export of foreign currency that arrived in Morocco through trade and payments of ransom. He also took steps to halt imports of foreign manufactured goods and to promote the production of similar goods in Morocco, bringing Flemish, Dutch and Italian artisans to teach Moroccans their trades in specially built workshops. A series of measures was also taken to attract merchants, especially from the Protestant countries of Northern Europe. In addition, al-Mansur established gunpowder factories and foundries for the production of artillery components, which Morocco had previously been forced to import from abroad. Steps were also taken to increase the cultivation of sugar cane through the building of refineries controlled by the *makhzen*, which also exploited the copper mines and salt resources.

Most of these measures served to enrich only the sultan and his dependants in government and thus were not generally welcomed and, on occasion, led to criticism or even rebellion. In 1583, two Jazuliyya *shaykhs* led a revolt against al-Mansur from their *zawiyas* in the Atlas mountains, complaining that the sugar refineries that the sultan was exploiting so successfully to serve the Christian nations contracted to buy the sugar left little land for the local inhabitants to farm for themselves. Al-Mansur's response was to send an army of four thousand soldiers to crush the revolt. The two *shaykhs* were flayed alive and their skins, stuffed with straw, were placed on public display in Marrakesh. In a similar case in 1588, a living saint – or charlatan, as he was called after his beheading – called Ibn Qarqush, a religious leader who claimed to perform miracles and to be divinely guided, proclaimed himself Commander of the Faithful (*amir al mu'minin*) in the Habt region, where he built up a strong following. Ahmad al-Mansur resorted to religious propaganda as well as military action in his efforts to crush this rebellion. In the following year, there were other rebellions in Tuwat and Gurara, where local leaders appointed by Marrakesh attempted to gain independence through armed revolt. Once the revolts had been quelled, some members of the rebellious tribes were assigned permanent military service and obliged to leave the area. The chroniclers pass over these events very quickly, though al-Ifrani would not refrain from writing that Ahmad al-Mansur 'was greedy for the blood of his subjects' and did not hesitate to shed it. It is also al-Ifrani who includes in his chronicle a little story that tells a lot about the extent of force and violence exerted by the sovereign for the internal peace of the country as well as the regard with which he viewed his subjects: one day, al-Ifrani tells us, the great judge of Fez, Abdelwahid al-Humaydi, was travelling with a group of distinguished notables and jurists from Fez to the capital city of Marrakesh to participate in some religious ceremonies at the court of al-Mansur. During the journey, they met a line of convicts chained to one another, among whom there were women, marching with their guardians. In the moment in which al-Humaydi and his companions crossed the sorry line one of the woman prisoners went into labour and gave birth to a child there, in chains, in the middle of the fields. Al-Humaydi was shocked and pained by this spectacle and when he reached Marrakesh, he told the sultan about it with great reproach. Ahmad al-Mansur went into a fearful fit of anger and said: 'If you had not seen what you have seen, neither you nor your companions could travel and come here in peace and security, because the people of the Maghreb are madmen whose madness can only be dealt with in chains and locks.' Al-Humaydi was spared punishment because he had been a tutor of Ahmad al-Mansur when the sultan was very young.

From the beginning of his reign Ahmad al-Mansur was forced to devote much of his energy to maintaining an unstable peace within his kingdom, without ever being able to achieve total cohesion or to gain complete acceptance of his power and person. A number of the rebellions against him were certainly caused by the harsh tax burden he imposed on his subjects. But they were also related to the nature of local authority in the different regions of the country, split between the tribal chiefs and the *shaykhs* of Sufi brotherhoods on the one hand and the sultan's appointed military administrators and governors on the other. The sultan's men were not always seen as necessary or convenient by locals – especially given the price in taxes that their presence demanded. What advantages could they bring that were not already provided by traditional local authorities? What sort of compatibility could there be between the forms of local authority and those of the new *makhzen* of Ahmad al-Mansur?

This was a perpetual dilemma that was often resolved by force of arms. It was also negotiated through personal alliances, favours, donations. At the same time, it also required an enormous legitimizing effort. Al-Mansur had to carry out a series of propaganda activities which, together with the fear his armies inspired, helped to bring about the adherence, recognition, love and loyalty of his subjects. Conducive to that loyalty was fear, fear not only of the sultan himself but of the uncertain world in which they lived. Morocco felt besieged by enemies and Moroccans were very much aware of the vulnerability of their country. They were afraid of the Turks, of the Christians, of uncontrollable periods of drought, hunger and pestilence. They were sensitive, therefore, to propaganda that presented the sultan as a saviour.

Loyalty, love, absolute submission were emotions that the Sufi *shaykhs* could instil among their local communities. There was already, then, a model of authority that the sultan could not ignore. He had to devise a system that would include and give new meaning to political symbols already in circulation; in other words he could imbue popular ideas of Sufism with political content. Thus, the incorporation and support of the Sufi brotherhoods was fundamental, as was the absorption of their symbolic capital, the signs and messages that Sufism had diffused throughout every level and region of Moroccan society.

Al-Mansur transformed his capital Marrakesh into a veritable *zawiya*. There one could find the tombs and shrines of the most important Shadhiliyya *shaykhs* (in particular, that of Abd al-Karim al-Fellah) and of the main branch, the Jazuliyya: indeed, the tomb of al-Jazuli himself was in Marrakesh (his body was brought there by al-Mansur's brother and predecessor) as well as those of his successors in the leadership of the order, al-Ghazwani and al-Tabba. These tombs are still visited by pilgrims in Marrakesh today. Al-Mansur also initiated the building of a mosque and *madrasa* complex (completed by his son Abu Faris in 1605 and still one of the most important historical buildings in the city) above the tomb of another famous figure, Abu l-Abbas al-Sabti (d. 1130), one of the most renowned Moroccan Sufi saints, who was made the patron of Marrakesh.

MARRAKESH: THE CAPITAL CITY AND THE PALACE

Marrakesh was the physical embodiment of al-Mansur's political and economic reforms, but also the focus of his efforts to construct political legitimacy and an imperial ideology. He went to great lengths to improve and embellish his capital city, and to provide it with grandiose structures that, according to the sources, gave it a grandeur of a kind that had seldom been seen. In a country where former royal capitals (especially Fez) existed, his aim was to create a capital city that would be the political and economic centre of the country, furnished with all the trappings of power. Al-Mansur provided examples and advised his officers and officials on building fine houses and adorning them with beautiful gardens and orchards. To make this possible, he supervised a programme of canal-building and the construction of large-scale waterworks.

He also made great efforts to attract foreign merchants by offering them economic facilities, as well as free housing and physical protection; large houses built for their safety were to be fortified with walls dotted with sentry boxes manned by soldiers from the sultan's own guard. These security measures show, importantly, that the foreign merchants were not generally welcomed by the local population. Antonio de Saldanha, the captive Portuguese nobleman, wrote:

> In the streets set aside for their shops, all the goods of France, Italy, England and Spain were sold at lower prices than in the lands where they were produced . . . the town of Marrakesh then attained such greatness as it had never attained before nor ever would again . . .

> And to make certain of all this greatness and commerce, the sultan wrote to the Queen of England, to Flanders, France, Italy and Spain, and to the Duke of Medinasidonia and requested from them that which he desired, which was first-class officials in all the arts. And they were sent to him and they came to the Sharif because of the generosity with which he conducted himself in these affairs.

He brought more than two thousand captives from Fez, most of them Portuguese combatants taken at the battle of Alcazar. Houses and a hospital were built for these captives,

> and there is no doubt that many of them ceased to remember their Christian lands, and if they could ever have been certain that the life

of the Sharif were to be a long one, none of them would have wanted to
go back home because they could not have lived there with such
largesse nor at such discretion as here . . . because they all lived as they
pleased without anyone coming to bother them.

Saldanha's comments are interesting because they reveal the general
feeling that everything done in Morocco depended on the personal
will, and the continued good health, of the Sultan. The general perception was that there was nothing to guarantee continuity after his
death. Saldanha clearly admired the sultan and recorded that al-
Mansur, aware that a kingdom's prosperity depended on its ability to
manufacture its own products and export them, established all manner of workshops and factories in Marrakesh. Some, as mentioned
previously, were used for the founding of artillery pieces and the
manufacture of gunpowder, others to make guns, swords and horse
reins. There were also factories specializing in glazed faience wares
and tiles, and pharmacies where liquids were distilled and remedies
produced. Saldanha writes, 'All these workshops were directed by
excellent English, Flemish and French masters, and their workmen
were boys who had been captured at the time of Alcazar and assigned
to his own house by the sharif.' The old Jewish quarter, the Mellah
of Marrakesh, was teeming with life and activity.

It is thanks to Saldanha that we know that al-Mansur showed great
interest in the characteristics of and progress on the palace that Philip
II was building for himself at El Escorial as a setting for the display of
the power of the Spanish crown around the tombs of his dynastic predecessors. A desire for emulation was already behind al-Mansur's
decision to build funerary monuments to his forebears, in imitation
of the Mamluk tombs he had visited in Cairo during his years of exile.
In 1592, he also decided to undertake the building of a mosque that
would compete with the heroic monuments of a previous age. To pre-
pare for the task, al-Mansur sent agents to measure the Qarawiyyin
Mosque in Fez, the Zaytuna in Tunis and the Great Mosque of
Istanbul (Hagia Sophia). Foundations were laid for the grandiose
building in the Jamaa al-Fna' of Marrakesh, but the mosque was

never completed: al-Mansur's sudden death and the subsequent war of succession between his sons made further construction impossible.

Saldanha's interesting remarks about al-Mansur's fascination with the Escorial are highly significant. Two fundamental events that took place in 1492 – the discovery of America and the end of the *Reconquista* – had led the Spanish monarchy to believe that it was granted a special function of metaphysical origin, the leadership of the nation chosen by God to realize the very greatest political and spiritual undertakings. This pair of remarkable and near-simultaneous achievements was attributed to a divine providence that would be followed by the conversion of all humanity to the Christian faith and the re-establishment of the early Church. One of Philip II's most ostentatious titles was 'King of Jerusalem', revealing the Spanish crown's intention to rule all the holy places, to govern the whole of Christendom. Philip, a 'new Solomon', planned a representation of the recovery of the Hebrew monarchy of the Old Testament at El Escorial. The building was designed in accordance with biblical descriptions of the Temple of Solomon, taken as a model for construction because it was divine architecture inspired by God. It is impossible to know how much of this was known to Ahmad al-Mansur and his informants, but he must have realized the general importance of El Escorial as a means of legitimizing Philip's ambitions for universal empire. He also knew of the Topkapi, the palatial complex build by the Ottomans in Istanbul as both a setting for and an emblem of their imperial power.

Thus it was that Ahmad al-Mansur built his own palace, or, rather, his palatial complex of buildings, known as the *Dar al-Makhzen*. He built it with the intention of showing that his own sharifian dynasty was superior to any that had ruled Morocco before. Work began in December 1578; the best architects and artisans, many of them from Italy, were sought out and paid generously. The palace was built of marble brought from Carrara, paid for with its equivalent weight in Moroccan sugar (the deal was mentioned by Montaigne in his account of his voyage to Italy). Black and white marbles were used as a base for inlaid decoration in onyx and hard stones of every colour, and the marble capitals were gilded. The walls were plastered with tiles with intertwined floral and vegetable motifs, and others that simulated rich embroidery on silk coats. The upper tile panels contained calligraphed inscriptions in stucco of specially commissioned works by court poets that exalted the beauty of the site and the merits of its patron, just as at the Alhambra palace in Granada. This was a palace with a voice.

Ahmad al-Mansur was immensely proud of his palace and celebrated its inauguration lavishly in 1594. Arabic sources state that the palace was more magnificent than anything that had ever existed in Baghdad or Damascus, and that it also surpassed the legendary palace of Madinat al-Zahra' built by the Umayyads outside Cordoba. These Arabic sources emphasize in particular the construction and characteristics of the palace of al-Badi' ('the Incomparable', one of the names of God) and the various celebrations that took place within it, especially the *Mawlid*, the celebration of the birthday of the Prophet Muhammad. This feast was celebrated in Sufi milieus, and by Ahmad al-Mansur's time had acquired a clear political significance. There was also a clear link between court ceremonial and architecture: the sources dwell on the ceremonies and lavishness of the celebrations, but also on the pomp and pageantry with which the sultan travelled and received visitors in audience.

When the sultan granted an audience, he would conceal himself behind a *sitr* or veil. This practice, which had Abbasid and Fatimid precedents, had been adopted by al-Mansur's Ottoman contemporaries. Veiling symbolized the process of the caliph's evanescence, the final objective being disappearance – *ghayba* – an absence in order to be omnipresent. The *sitr* signalled an unbridgeable gap between the caliph and the rest of humanity, his exceptional status as *khalifat Allah*, 'representative of God' (as distinct from the more usual caliphal title, *khalifat rasul Allah*, 'representative of the Prophet of God'), in which capacity he was everywhere present, aware of everything that was going on. Some *'ulama* rejected these practices as casting the caliph in a semi-divine role, as can be seen in the account

of the audience with Ahmad Baba al-Timbukti, the renowned
Sudanese *'alim* who was captured and taken before al-Mansur in his
palace in Marrakesh. Al-Mansur received Ahmad Baba sitting behind
the curtain that always separated him from the public. On witnessing
the preparations, Ahmad Baba said, 'God, blessed and extolled, has
declared in the Qur'an that no human being can communicate with
God if it is not through revealed Law or by staying hidden behind a
veil: you imitate then the supreme Lord [God]; but if you wish to
speak with me, put aside the curtain and come towards me.' This
anecdote, a *post facto* reconstruction of the well-known theme of the
wise man or saint who rebukes a ruler, was a means of expressing
the deep discomfort of the *'ulama* with the sultan's attempts at self-
glorification.

The palace of al-Badi' was destroyed by Muley Isma'il in 1610
during the civil war fought by Ahmad al-Mansur's heirs, but detailed
descriptions of it have survived in the accounts of contemporary
court chroniclers and European travellers, some of whom even
included maps and drawings; one of the most important is conserved
at the library of El Escorial. It was situated within the confines of
the Almohad *qasbah* – one way in which al-Mansur sought to
present himself as an incarnation of the living past. Within the
vast complex of buildings of the Dar al-Makhzen, the palace of
al-Badi' was reserved exclusively for receptions and ceremonies. It
comprised a rectangular courtyard with two domes (*qubbatayn*) at
each end. The courtyard enclosed a symmetrical *riyad*, or internal
garden, built on two axes that divided it into four sections with a
pond for breeding fish at the centre; the latter was fed by canals
bringing clear, fresh and ceaselessly flowing water down from the
Atlas mountains. The plan was of ancient Persian origin, seen nearer
to Ahmad's time and place in the Court of the Lions in the Alhambra
of Granada.

In the garden, the sultan planted many varieties of fertile fruit
trees and a great number of palm trees which were subjected to such
successful grafting that they began to yield prodigious quantities of
fruit after only five or six years. Descriptions of the garden reflect the

passage in the Qur'an (55:46–78) on the Gardens of Paradise, which were also divided into four, served by streams and adorned by many varieties of fruit trees.

It was a design of clearly divine inspiration, of architecture revealed or inspired directly by God. It was said that the fruits of the garden of al-Badiʻ, such as the miraculous dates that appeared even before the palm trees had reached their proper height, could not be transported to Spain because, once there, they rotted immediately: like fruits of Paradise, they could not be enjoyed by infidels. The garden of al-Badiʻ was not of course the first garden designed along these lines with legitimizing intentions. Among those who had carried out such projects in the past was the Cordoban caliph, the Umayyad Abd al-Rahman III, in his palace of Madinat al-Zahra', at a time of great rivalry with the Fatimids for the caliphate.

The *qubba* used for receptions was built on two levels with an internal staircase, so that the interior of the palace was conceived as a sort of monumental platform or theatrical stage for the *sharif*'s appearances. Descriptions of al-Badiʻ are accompanied by accounts of the fabulous celebrations with which al-Mansur marked the feast of the *Mawlid*. These were elaborate and solemn celebrations, intended more to exalt the figure of the caliph rather than his forebear, the Prophet Muhammad, but certainly orchestrated to emphasize the link between the former and the latter.

The *Mawlid* celebrations at al-Badiʻ, in which all the classes and hierarchies of the realm participated in order of their social importance, amazed the participants and spectators, even the *sharifs*, *qadi*s, holy men and viziers, 'all of whom were able to imagine that they were in the gardens of Paradise'. Paradise, for Muslims, is also organized hierarchically.

> Dressed in beautiful clothing that emphasized even more his majestic and imposing appearance, the sultan sat in his usual place. He was contemplated with respect and admiration. His dazzling beauty struck all those present; men of the country and inhabitants of the city alike felt great pleasure as they looked upon him.

Al-Tamagruti, an influential courtier, ambassador and official chronicler, insisted repeatedly that all those present believed themselves to be in Paradise. When describing the great quantities of food offered at these occasions, al-Tamagruti explains that, as in Paradise, guests were able to eat as much as they wanted without fear of evil.

According to al-Ifrani, another of al-Mansur's official historians, one leading courtier exclaimed during the celebration, 'If I knew, my Lord, that there were one who loved you more than I do, I would cease to consider myself as belonging to the community of Muslims.' Love for the sultan became identified with love for God and with belonging or not to the *umma*, the community of believers.

The festival of the breaking of the fast of Ramadan was also described in great detail by official chroniclers. For this event, the sultan appeared dressed in white, mounted on a white horse and surrounded by his personal guard, who held a parasol over his head, revealing himself as half-saint, half-warrior. The parasol, originally a Buddhist symbol of divinity, was used by various Muslim rulers, including the Fatimids, and symbolized closeness to God. Al-Tamagruti writes that when the sultan presented himself in this way, he brought to mind a mountain of clemency and goodness, or a lion full of heroism and courage (*asad*, 'lion', was one of the appellatives of Ali, the son-in-law of the Prophet, husband of Fatima) in a sea of generosity and forgiveness, or a full moon spreading the clarity of its light through the darkness of the night. All of these are stock themes in Arabic, especially Andalusian, poetry. At the same time, these metaphors have strong messianic associations that hark back to the titles and terms used by Abbasid caliphs, thereby reinforcing the idea of continuity and the incorporation of a glorious past. Another recurring theme is the sultan's generosity and the manner in which he distributed gifts of gold and silver. Accounts of al-Mansur's generosity are reminiscent of the *hadith*, often invoked by, among others, al-Ifrani, which reads 'At the end of my community there will be a caliph who will pour out money without counting it.' Such generosity was often compared to rain-bearing clouds. This theme also reappears in the inscription on a marble fountain that al-Mansur donated to the Qarawiyyin Mosque in Fez in 999/1588, where the sultan is described as a sea of generosity. Generosity is a recurring subject: the extent of his generosity matched perceptions of the extent of his power. The sultan had obligations towards his vassals and his elites, and the measure of his capacity to exercise power was his dispatching of these duties with generosity. Silver and gold were not only capital but symbols of power.

The pomp associated with al-Mansur's official journeys became one of the essential rituals of Moroccan dynastic power from then on. It was not only related to the official function of such journeys, during which taxes were collected from different provinces within the sultan's territory and allegiances from the tribes were renewed. It also served to express a means of exercising power, and created a mise en scène designed to meet the expectations of the sultan's subjects. This setting made use of symbols that communicated the concepts of dynastic and religious continuity with previous Islamic sovereigns, and above all suggested a true mimesis of the Prophet and his Companions. There was no ceremony or ritual that did not include a vindication of the blood ties between the Prophet and al-Mansur, for, as was stated in the inscription on the mausoleum that al-Mansur built for his mother, 'The Prophet of God has said: all genealogy is my lineage. Every son of a woman has his father as agnate, except the sons of Fatima, who have me as their father and as agnate.' In his correspondence with both Muslim and Christian authorities, one of the titles Ahmad al-Mansur used was that of 'al-Fatimi', descendant of Fatima. In the Maghreb, this appellative was (and still is) equivalent to the term *Mahdi*, the Islamic messiah.

The emphasis on the special link between Ahmad and the Prophet Muhammad is revealed in official accounts through the descriptions of festivals and ceremonies, and also in accounts devoted to, for example, listing all the rebels crushed by al-Mansur. These accounts of defeated rivals transform the idea of *fitna* (or internal strife) into a positive element in a history that enhanced the sultan's standing by allowing his subjects to perceive him as reproducing the Prophet's great exploits – disorder was the domain of the Jahiliyya (the time of

Ignorance before the arrival of Islam) and its defeat an essential aspect of the monarch's legitimacy. From the battle of Alcazar, which the chronicles equate with the battle of Badr, one of the most famous battles won by the Prophet, the descriptions of al-Mansur's feats of arms are cast as repeating the gestes of the Prophet.

Fitna or disorder was also a warning of the End of Time, when the Awaited *Imam*, the *Mahdi*, would come. The sultan based his claims on his sharifian lineage and direct descent from the Prophet in order to establish the holy nature of his reign, and to attempt to unfold the extraordinary nature of his divine sanction. But, despite all the endeavours of official historians, supported by the palace chancellery, al-Mansur's claim to power was always of a dubious legitimacy, as indicated by various other aspirants to the caliphate from within his own family, such as Muley al-Nasr, brother of sultan Muhammad al-Mutawakkil, who had been forced to flee to Spain when his father's attempts at revolt failed but who later returned to challenge Ahmad al-Mansur, or Abd al-Malik's son exiled in Algeria. Ahmad al-Mansur pre-empted further rebellions by imprisoning all his nephews, the *sharifs* of Marrakesh, and ordering their eyes to be put out, an alternative approach to that of the Ottoman sultans, who strangled their brothers upon their ascent to the throne.

Jihad was also an important ingredient in al-Mansur's political discourse. We have seen that *jihad* was the alleged motive for his conquest of the Sudan. We have also seen his cherished wish to conquer Andalusia. And yet, al-Mansur never launched an attack against any of the Iberian strongholds on the Moroccan coast. He never attempted to recover Tangier or Ceuta or Melilla or Oran. One wonders if part of this discourse was directed at certain groups, especially his Morisco army, to prevent them from organizing their own campaigns and to gain their emotional support. After all, he began his reign by quelling an attempted coup by his Andalusian troops. *Jihad* was also a main part of a messianic discourse. Al-Mansur's claims on *jihad* always insist that it can only be launched under the leadership of the *imam*, the singular head of the Muslim community, and that he was, indeed, the Commander of the Faithful.

BELIEF IN THE *MAHDI*

Ahmad's father and the founder of the Sa'dian dynasty, Muhammad al-Shaykh, promoted the idea that he was the *Mahdi* with the help of Sufi brotherhoods. The *Mahdi*, the Rightly Guided One, the Islamic messiah, must, according to messianic lore, be a descendant of the Prophet Muhammad, who will come at the End of Time to restore the purity of the early faith and establish justice on earth until the Final Hour. The Islamic messiah embodies the aspirations of his followers to restore the faith, just as it was experienced during the life of the Prophet, by bringing divine and uncorrupted guidance to all humankind, and by establishing a social order that is fair and free from all oppression, an order that will precede the End of Times. Salvation in the form of return to that infinitely pure past is provided by a redeemer who acts as a mediator between the human and the divine, who will impose the law of Islam on the whole of humankind, bringing with it a state of pure harmony before the End.

That is to say, the *Mahdi* will be a restorer and renewer of religion, and also the man through whom the redemption of the community of believers will be carried out. He will lead the final *jihad*: he will fight and vanquish the *Dajjal*, the Islamic Anti-Christ. He is an avatar of Muhammad and therefore the only and true *imam* of the community, the legitimate caliph, God's lieutenant on earth, divinely inspired and guided by God. For followers of movements arising around the figure of a *Mahdi* – quite common in the history of the Maghreb – the only possible caliph is the *Mahdi*. But the opposite is also true – there has rarely been a claim to the caliphate in Moroccan history that did not begin with messianic propaganda.

The spread of Sufism in the Maghreb contributed powerfully to the spread of apocalyptic expectations in popular milieus, instilling a desire for purification and regeneration as well as divinely inspired guidance. Several Sufi orders, especially the Jazuliyya, which supported the Sa'di dynasty in its beginnings, maintained a state of messianic expectation that was fed by the ideas of prophetic illumination and divine inspiration associated with Sufism. Indeed, Ahmad al-Mansur's propaganda even used the vocabulary of mysticism, suffusing it with political meaning. Most significant is the use of the Sufi term *qutb*, 'pole' or 'axis', applied to the sultan. *Qutbaniyya* or paradigmatic sainthood was dominant in Moroccan mysticism throughout the sixteenth century: it referred to spiritual authority as an acquired property of the Sufi *shaykh* who best mirrored the qualities of the Prophet, and as an inborn grace transmitted by the Prophetic bloodline as expressed by *al-wiratha al-nabawiyya*, the 'Prophetic inheritance', another term often used by *shaykhs* of the Jazuliyya order and by the Sultan.

This sort of rhetoric gives the reigning sultan an eschatological identity in order to justify his supreme power and his universalizing imperial aspirations. A paradigm was designed that joined his claim to universal dominance with spiritual authority based on a holy lineage. Thus, Ahmad al-Mansur was the heir of the Prophet and of Prophecy, the only legitimate ruler for all Muslims. Those who did not obey him became heretics against whom it was permissible to fight. His apologists sought to present him as the renewer of religion (*mujaddid*), a revivalist figure with messianic appeal.

8

MESSIANISM AND THE RIVALRY WITH THE OTTOMANS

Messianism is a very powerful ideology. It serves dynastic power in the case of shaky or weakly established legitimacy, and is a powerful lever of the emotions of the underprivileged classes. In the Moroccan case, messianism nourished by Sufism heightened the sense of expectation of the advent of a saviour. Messianic expectations had been a marked feature of political and religious life in the Mediterranean area since the early sixteenth century. The context for a final, decisive confrontation between Christendom and Islam was provided, on the one hand, by the great Ottoman expansion and its symbolic high-point, the conquest of Constantinople by the Turks in 1453 and, on the other, by the Christian conquest of the entire territory of the Iberian Peninsula and the extension of such conquests into North Africa. All of these occurrences fed a general feeling that the messianic era was imminent.

On the Christian side, the military advances induced an intense wave of messianic enthusiasm that imagined the definitive end of Islam, the capture of Jerusalem, the re-establishment of the early Church and the conversion of all humankind to the Christian faith. In Iberia, such messianic zeal propelled the conquest and evangelization of America. The great Portuguese voyages of discovery were driven by the messianic quests to find the mythical kingdom of Prester John. On the Muslim side of the Mediterranean, messianic expectations were also nourished by the fact that the final decade of the sixteenth century coincided with the end of the tenth century of the Hijra, the Millennium in the Islamic calendar.

THE MILLENNIUM AND THE CONQUEST OF WESTERN SUDAN

As seen from Earth, the planets Saturn and Jupiter are aligned every 960 years, after travelling the entire course of the zodiac. This slowly recurring astronomical phenomenon, known as the 'great conjunction' or the 'auspicious conjunction', was discussed in eschatological texts that announced the end of an era, or a cyclical renewal manifested through signs and wonders, whether catastrophes like plague and drought, the appearance of a prophet sent 'with a proof of his divine mission', or the arrival of a 'great and powerful king'.

The Abbasid astrologer Abu Ma'shar (d. 886) produced a theory on the rise and fall of dynasties in accordance with the conjunction of the planets Jupiter and Saturn which led to the development of a number of apocalyptic movements. Abu Ma'shar's work was translated into Latin in Spain during the medieval period, and later into Castilian; he was known in the Iberian Peninsula as Abulmasar. Latin translations of his work were printed and reprinted in Rome and Venice at the beginning of the sixteenth century. His texts were interpreted in Iberia by sixteenth-century Muslims and Christians alike as announcing the arrival of the Anti-Christ at the time of the great conjunction due to occur in 990/1582. This conjunction acquired particularly strong apocalyptic connotations for Muslims because of its close proximity to the Islamic Millennium, between October 1591 and October 1592.

The texts were familiar to the Spanish Moriscos, who believed that they were witnessing the end of their own world during this period. This belief is mentioned in the work of Al-Suyuti (d. 1505), a widely read scholar who forecast the appearance of a renewer of religion (*mujaddid al-din*) at the beginning of the tenth *hijri* century. Al-Suyuti's description of this renewer of religion has much in common with the awaited *Mahdi*. Al-Suyuti evokes the apocalyptic fervour of the end of the century, writing that the fervour was shared by both learned and ordinary people, who quoted *hadiths* or Prophetic traditions that confirmed their belief that history would end with the coming of the tenth century. According to one of these traditions, the Prophet said that at the beginning of each new century God would send a man, a descendant of his family, who would explain matters of religion anew, a man who would bring about the renewal of religion. It so happens that the year 1000 of the Muslim Era was precisely the time of the Moroccan expedition to Sudan, an event that required a special effort of legitimation on the part of Ahmad al-Mansur's secretaries, officials and chroniclers.

Among the chroniclers, it is al-Ifrani who applied most intensely the 'renewer of religion' theme to the sultan. Al-Ifrani inserts the full texts of letters addressed to al-Mansur by different religious scholars into his chronicle; all of these scholars expound on the theme of the *mujaddid*, quoting *hadiths* about the renewer of religion, on how he would appear at the beginning of a century, and how the signs of his coming would be the defeat of *fitna* or internal strife, and Infidelity. Some of the scholars went even further, claiming that al-Mansur was the man to whom God had promised dominance over the whole world because of his resemblance to the *Mahdi*. Al-Ifrani explains the unquestionable eschatological character of Ahmad al-Mansur's reign, describing the signs that foretold his arrival:

> The entry of the sultan Ahmad al-Mansur's troops in Sudan, the capture of the sultan Askiya in his palace at Gao, and the conquest of Timbuktu and its region had been some of the numerous foretelling signs of the imminent coming of the *Mahdi*. Equally, the plague during these years, the seditions and the costliness of foodstuffs that still persists in some regions had been signs of the coming of the *Mahdi*, and to this list must be added the conquest of Oran [then in Spanish hands], which must be carried out by the *Mahdi* or under his orders.

From these texts, one might interpret al-Mansur's expedition to Western Sudan in 1591 as an attempt by the sultan to have himself seen as (or to become) the Universal Emperor of the Last Days, or as an attempt to legitimize an action contested by many of his own *'ulama* by having himself declared to be such.

In the surviving chronicles, the messianic discourse is emphatically linked to the conquest of Sudan. It was in the early stages of the conquest that those arguments were needed, so as to create a legitimate enterprise. In the letters sent out to various parts of the Moroccan realm to announce the news of al-Mansur's actions in Sudan, his court secretaries insisted that the dynasty had rightfully inherited the lands of the Prophet's descendants as caliphs of Islam and guides to the community. Al-Mansur was portrayed as the *Fatimi* and prophetic *imam* who had added another victory to his previous ones, that over Sudan, which prefigured the unity of Islam. These letters claimed that no dynasty since antiquity had been so powerful, or so dominant over such distant lands, and that this showed God's predilection for the dynasty. The caliph's banners, they said, had brought light to a dark horizon, his army resembling the column of dawn that pierces the darkness of night. The messianic image of the dissipation of darkness was linked here to the skin-colour of the defeated Sudanese armies, which became an image of evil and ignorance in a war between the sons of light and the sons of darkness. Who read these chronicles, and to whom they were addressed? The elites, no doubt, particularly the *'ulama*. But these letters, included in the chronicles as copies of those sent abroad, were also read by the *imams* in the mosques as part of the Friday sermon, and gathered a wide audience throughout the country. They were an important vehicle of propaganda.

The same apocalyptic tone was employed in the expression of the aim to reconquer al-Andalus for the Muslim faith, an action that, it was said, would be achieved one day by the awaited *Mahdi*. Al-Mansur wrote to renowned Egyptian *'ulama,* requesting them to lead prayers in Medina and Mecca to ask God to help him defeat the Enemy of Religion, and to lend him assistance to 'conquer al-Andalus, make the vestiges of Faith come alive again in that country, and resuscitate the vestiges of Islam'. In another letter written in very similar terms to the *sharif* Abu l-Mahasin Hasan, 'Sultan of Mecca and Medina', al-Mansur asked for the same spiritual assistance and support for his mission.

In Morocco the thirteenth-century *Kitab al-Tadhkira* by the Andalusi al-Qurtubi (the Cordoban) was widely read. It was popular especially in Sufi milieus, and consisted of a compendium of traditions, legends and poems about the appearance of the *Mahdi*, who was thought to be about to manifest himself in the Maghreb. According to al-Qurtubi, the *Mahdi* would organize an army with which he would cross the Strait of Gibraltar over a miraculous bridge and reconquer seventy cities from the Christians. After that, he would personally lead prayers in the mosque of Seville. This text was also cited by al-Mansur's court historians and in particular by al-Tamagruti, Moroccan ambassador to Istanbul in 1589–90.

For it was not only the conquest of Sudan that needed to be justified through the use of a messianic discourse. The political and symbolic rivalry of the Ottomans, who posed a constant threat to the Maghreb, was another reason for its deployment. In his account of his diplomatic mission to Istanbul, al-Tamagruti included a brief report on the origins of the Ottomans that served to introduce the argument that the monarchs of the Maghreb were superior to the Ottomans and possessed a unique, legitimate right to the caliphate, because unlike the Ottomans they were descendants of the Prophet and a caliphate could only be legitimate if held by a member of the Quraysh, the tribe of the Prophet. In al-Tamagruti's view, the Ottomans had no right to call themselves caliphs. He believed, or professed to believe, that it was the sovereigns of Morocco who should lead and govern all Muslims, and not the Ottoman sultan. Al-Tamagruti devoted several pages to citations from the *Tadhkira* of al-Qurtubi in support of this argument. In all, four pages of al-Tamagruti's text are devoted to recording traditions about the appearance of the *Mahdi*, his physical characteristics, how he would belong to the family of the Prophet through Fatima, how he would fill the world with justice, conquer Rome, Jerusalem and Istanbul, and so on. He then returns to describing Ahmad al-Mansur, who matches all the descriptions contained in the traditions he has just cited, even in his physical appearance, and explains how al-Mansur's victory in the Sudan shows that he has started to carry out his conquest of the world, where he will spread blessings, safety and fertility like benevolent rain.

Al-Tamagruti's text, in fact his whole argument, is very important. It was made use of much later, in the first decade of the twentieth century, when the Ottoman caliph declared that the war he was obliged to fight against Russia was a *jihad*, and therefore demanded a series of duties from all Muslims, wherever they happened to live. The first such duty was, of course, not to fight in the Russian army, or in that of any of its allies, such as France. Morocco was at that time a French protectorate, and the chief French official in Rabat, General Lyautey, asked the Moroccan *'ulama* to refute the Ottoman appeal with theological and juridical arguments. This request was duly met by the *'ulama*, but in extremely cautious terms: their *fatwa* affirmed that the legitimate caliph must be an Arab of *sharif* descent, and that the sultan of Morocco was thus better qualified for the title than the Turkish sovereign, provided that he was apt for it, meaning that he was not under the protection of a foreign Christian power. This *fatwa* was both equivocal and dangerous for the French position in Morocco, but it used, one by one, all of al-Tamagruti's original arguments.

The letters sent by al-Mansur to the *shurafa* of Medina and Mecca informed them of his military plans and asked for their spiritual assistance and support. Such support, he hoped, would also confer legitimacy. His strategy can be seen as even more significant if we consider that one of the most important titles held by the Ottoman sultan since the time of Selim I (r. 1512–20), who had declared himself caliph, was that of *khadim al-haramayn al-sharifayn*, guardian and defender of the holy places. In the same way that the European Holy Roman Emperor must preside over Rome, the caliph was the guardian of Mecca and Medina. Such titles gave legitimacy and primacy to the Ottomans, and to other Muslim rulers over time, and gave them power over the political and sacred essence of the caliphate. Caliphal claims lay behind the political activity and propaganda of the Ottomans in the Maghreb, and the Moroccan dynasty staked its own claims in direct opposition to them.

This explains why al-Tamagruti, in his account of his mission to Turkey, insisted so strongly on the indisputable right of the Moroccan dynasty to the caliphate and why, in what is essentially a report of diplomatic dealings in Istanbul, he used such a battery of arguments concerning the *Mahdi* and his appearance in the Far West. Al-Tamagruti found at the Ottoman court a new shared imperial culture transmitted by a corporate elite, a group of chroniclers and secretaries who had provided Sultan Suleyman the Lawgiver, or the Magnificent, with an almost sacred status. These thinkers had also overseen the formulation of a visual and literary imperial iconography whose aim was the monopolization of temporal and spiritual authority, and the ideological legitimization of that monopoly. This elite was to find in messianism the ultimate recipe for reconciling a number of competing intellectual, social and political trends. It was all of this that Sultan Ahmad al-Mansur would try to emulate.

MOROCCAN RIVALRY WITH THE OTTOMANS

The legitimizing and propagandistic efforts of Ahmad al-Mansur take on an added dimension if we consider similar efforts also made by Ottoman sovereigns. In the early sixteenth century, the Islamic nations in the Eastern Mediterranean, particularly the Ottoman Empire, found themselves, like the Islamic regions in the West, facing increasingly aggressive Christian powers, as well as the new Safavid state in Iran. Ottoman dynastic legitimacy was at this time far from being commonly accepted. In Iran, a group known as the *Qizilbash* (Red Heads) had taken up arms at the very beginning of the sixteenth century in favour of their divinely inspired leader, Shaykh Isma'il al-Safavi (1501–24), the *shaykh* of a Sufi brotherhood who was expected by his followers to establish the realm of justice on earth. The Safavids were Shi'ites and believed in the divine power of their *imam*.

Sultan Selim (r. 1512–20) was to take his place in Ottoman historiography as one of the great conquerors of the dynasty. According to sixteenth-century historians, if it had not been for his premature death, he would have become a conqueror on the scale of a Chingiz Khan or Alexander the Great, and would have shown the falseness of Safavid, and therefore Shi'ite, claims of divine inspiration and divine support for their cause. Selim was said to be the *mujaddid* of the tenth century, the renewer of religion divinely enabled to set right the world of Islam. Selim's most eloquent claim to this status was based on the fact that he had defeated Shah Isma'il in 1512. In the chronicles written by his courtiers, Selim is described as the *Mahdi* of the Last Days and Divine Force (*qudrat-i ilahi*), as well as a second Alexander, the World Conqueror whose coming at the End of Time had been foretold by apocalyptic literature dating from the early Islamic period. The Ottoman–Safavid rivalry and Selim's military accomplishments were retold in an apocalyptic interpretative mode. Selim and his court also participated in the process of shaping Ottoman sovereignty to a messianic model through the use of the imagery and terminology of the religious and military brotherhoods.

The link between Ottoman imperial ideology and messianism reached its peak in the years after 1520, when Suleyman the Magnificent ascended the throne. The first thirty of the fifty years of his rule were to become a sacralized and exemplary period in the writings of Ottoman historians, the apex of their history. The emphasis placed from the beginning of his reign by Suleyman himself, and by his chroniclers, on the idea that his reign would be a time of perfect, impartial justice constituted an apocalyptic gesture intended to show that his age, the tenth century of the Muslim era, was in fact the Millennium, and to suggest that he was the ruler who would fill the world with justice as it had previously been filled with injustice. The main theme was Suleyman's rivalry with the Habsburg Emperor

Charles V of Spain: both were seen as aspirants to the status of divinely guided universal ruler or Last World Emperor.

Historians of Suleyman's period set out an impressive array of arguments in his favour: that he was the *mujaddid* was indicated in so many ways, among them the astral conjunctions for the year 960/1522–3. They wrote that Suleyman was the *sahib qiran* or Master of the Great Conjunction, in reference to the notion of the universal ruler who would usher in the dominion of one single religion at the time of the great conjunction of the stars. Suleyman was to be imagined as the spiritual ruler of the world, uniting in his person both temporal and spiritual powers.

Suleyman allowed himself to be spoken of and described as the Last World Emperor; he even played an active role in the formation of his messianic image and seems to have believed in his own apocalyptic role. If Charles V was the heir and conqueror of Rome, sacked by his troops in 1527, Suleyman argued that his own capital, Istanbul, was the true inheritor of the essence of the Roman Empire. The symbolic function of Constantinople as a second Rome became so important that when Suleyman achieved his conquest of the Danube valley, he even ordered engraved images of himself to be distributed that depicted him wearing the Papal tiara. The tiara was intended to show the world that the Ottoman emperors were the true heirs of the Roman Empire through Byzantium.

From the age of about sixty, Suleyman's health began to deteriorate. His dreams of universal dominion had not been fulfilled, his sons disputed the succession and, equally importantly, the time of the Millennium had passed. Thus it was that the 'classic' Ottoman historiography of the second half of the reign lost all its messianic connotations. However, it is clear that Suleyman's sovereignty was initially formulated within the powerful prophetic and messianic currents of its time, and that it nourished itself on them. The apocalyptic content of Suleyman's ideology was related to his ability to bring about important, large-scale changes in society and the Ottoman order, projected as universal and ideal. The Turkish sultan's legal innovations were founded on the assumptions of both his popular and elite subjects that the sultan had an authority over the interpretation and mandate of the law that was concomitant with his messianic nature. The tremendous energy liberated by messianic expectations led to the legitimization of an absolute power, but also to the legitimization of changes and innovations that could have been the cause of a rupture with the established order, even when these changes, as in the case of Suleyman, were instituted from within the establishment and not in revolt against it.

Ahmad al-Mansur also implemented measures that brought about profound changes and with which he sought to make his own stand against the pressure and rivalry of the Spanish Habsburgs on the one hand and the Ottomans on the other. Both rivals had, as we have seen, their own aspirations to the title of Last World Emperor. The ideology that transpires in the historiography of Ahmad al-Mansur was able to feed on the same prophetic and messianic currents that Selim and above all Suleyman had captured, and which had been spread through the popular classes thanks to the powerful role of the Sufi brotherhoods. The work of these historians also shows up the clear political and symbolic rivalry of the Moroccan dynasty with the Ottomans and the wish to counterbalance the permanent and real danger of Turkish intervention in the Maghreb. Faced with the opposition of a powerful and conservative class of interpreters of the law, the kind of innovation or 'modernization' that al-Mansur wished to bring to so many areas of political and social life stood in need of some sort of messianic vindication. Processes of reform undertaken by those in power needed a mahdist justification.

PLAGUE, HUNGER AND WAR

In claiming for himself the role of Last World Emperor, Ahmad was claiming for himself not only superiority to the Ottomans in his foreign policy, but the same authority to transform the government of Morocco. After 1595, cracks began to appear in the edifice constructed by Ahmad al-Mansur. High levels of taxation kept large numbers of people in poverty, and years of drought and bad harvests led to a plague epidemic that began to pummel the country hard from 1598. According to reports by English merchants from the first months of that year, some 230,000 people had died and were buried on the outskirts of Marrakesh, from which the sultan fled to live in a tent in open land. In the months that followed, the merchants estimated that around thirty thousand people died every single day. Al-Mansur wrote to his sons to recommend that they leave the cities and live in tents in the country, moving frequently from one site to another. He also recommended a whole array of prophylactic measures – which proved not to be of any use for himself.

At the height of the epidemic, al-Mansur learned that his son Muley al-Shaykh, the crown prince, had rebelled against him with the intention of taking his throne. In addition, Muley al-Shaykh had sought to further his cause by negotiating with Spain, with a view to making a joint attack on the Ottomans in Algeria: al-Shaykh was worried that the Ottomans would support an alternative Moroccan candidate (his first cousin, Muley Isma'il, Abd al-Malik's son) to the throne that he believed he should rightfully inherit from his father. Muley al-Shaykh's actions took place at the same time as his father Ahmad al-Mansur was concluding a peace deal with the Ottomans. Al-Mansur sent some of the most reputed *'ulama* of his court to convince his son to abandon the path of rebellion, and to offer him the governorship of Sijilmassa. It was to no avail. And so, in October 1602, Ahmad al-Mansur left Marrakesh at the head of his army to fight against his own son, whom he successfully defeated and who was arrested and imprisoned in the city of Meknes.

The same *'ulama* urged al-Mansur to have his son put to death, but he refused. Khayzuran, his wife and mother of al-Shaykh, interceded in his favour. Instead, al-Mansur placed another son, Muley Zidan, in his brother's post as governor of Fez, and a third, Abu Faris, was awarded the position of governor of Marrakesh. Ahmad al-Mansur never stripped his eldest son of his title of crown prince, despite having thrown him into prison.

Ahmad al-Mansur never returned to his capital after defeating al-Shaykh, but died of the plague while on the outskirts of Fez with his army in August 1603. He was buried in Fez, in a very simple ceremony, on the day he died. His body would later be transported to Marrakesh, where he is buried with his forebears. Both his burial and his funeral were devoid of pomp and ceremonial and very much in contrast with those of his life-long rival Philip II, who organized his own spectacular burial and funeral and even presided over the rehearsals.

Ahmad al-Mansur's death left the country in a state of confusion. His two younger sons, Muley Zidan and Abu Faris, each had a powerful army of his own and could rely on support from a number of the elites in the country. Like their father, they had also established their own ties with clans and families, their own clientele and vassals. Each brother refused to accept the claims of the other, and the country was divided into two separate kingdoms, with capitals in Fez and Marrakesh. Lack of agreement between them led to the freeing of Muley al-Shaykh, who became a third contender for the throne. War broke out between the three factions, a bloody civil war that was to last for almost a decade, sowing chaos that was intensified by the interference of foreign powers: the Ottomans and the Dutch supported Muley Zidan, whereas Muley al-Shaykh received help from Spain, where he took refuge after his release from prison. In his temporary exile in Carmona, al-Shaykh played on the Spanish fears of Ottoman annexation of Morocco as a result of the victory of Zidan, the Ottoman candidate. Al-Shaykh offered the port of Larache to Philip III, who agreed to the transfer of the port in exchange for 200,000 ducats plus a loan of six thousand soldiers, which permitted al-Shaykh to return to Morocco. This transfer eventually took place in 1610, when Larache was occupied by the Spaniards.

In the meantime, al-Shaykh sent his own son, Abdallah, to attack Marrakesh; he succeeded in conquering the city and subjected it to a bloody round of looting and pillage. The city of Marrakesh, centre and emblem of Ahmad al-Mansur's power, was thoroughly sacked and destroyed in 1609. John Smith, an English merchant who first visited the city after 1610, wrote the following words in his *Relation* of that visit, more expressive than any others of the final outcome of Ahmad's imperial ambitions:

> [Marrakesh] for the most part, is defaced, but by the many pinnacles and towers with balls on their tops, hath much appearance of much sumptuosnesse and curiositie . . . the houses in most parts lye tumbled one above another, the walls of earth are with the great fresh flouds washed to the ground . . . Strange tales they will tell of a great garden wherein were all sorts of birds, fishes, beasts, fruits and fountaines which for beautie, art and pleasure exceeded any place knowne in the world though now nothing but dunghils, pigeonhouses, shrubs and bushes. There are yet many excellent fountaines, adorned with marble, and many arches, pillers, towers, ports and temples; but most only reliques of lamentable ruines and sad desolation.

CONCLUSION

In this book we have come to know relatively little about al-Mansur's private life. Of the many complex and often contradictory features that go to make up a personality the reader gets scarcely a glimpse. Indeed, it is only Ahmad al-Mansur's works and public conduct that are documented in this biography. The fact is that our sources simply will not allow us to get inside al-Mansur: they tell nothing about his gestures, thoughts, habits, doubts, dilemmas or his personal and family relationships. Inhabitants of the early modern Maghreb never cared to make private affections and emotions publicly known. They do refer to his generosity and his terrible outbursts of anger, but then both of these were characteristics of public importance. His unalterability and inscrutability were perceived as signs of power that intimidated those in his presence so acutely that they were left literally speechless.

Arabic sources, then, do not inform us about those aspects of intimate and family life that comprised the private essence of Ahmad al-Mansur. European sources are equally silent, as contemporary European informers could not access the ruler's private sphere. Nor, it seems, were they curious. Al-Mansur's European contemporaries were not as interested in Muslim family life, or the private lives of public figures, as we are now. For this reason, it has not been possible for me to determine the names of his wives, or how many children he had – we know only of those sons who played a public role, and the names of their mothers. Indeed it is as mothers, not wives, that al-Mansur's spouses are present in the sources at all.

In coming to know al-Mansur, I would have liked to be able to draw on something equivalent to the huge surviving personal correspondence between Philip II of Spain and his two favourite daughters, Catalina Micaela and Isabel Clara Eugenia. Ahmad al-Mansur must have written many letters to his children, but the lack of Moroccan archives for early modern times has meant that the only letters to survive are those which the chroniclers perceived as politically relevant or useful for establishing the chronological order of events, and which they therefore included in their chronicles.

Al-Mansur's personality must have been contradictory and complex. This is the conclusion one reaches from a study of his political measures. They reveal a person struggling between tradition and modernity, a struggle that must have created not a few personal dilemmas. But it is not my intention to summarize here the personal characteristics of intelligence, political skill or prudence or to repeat the portrayal of al-Mansur as the wise, pious and brave soldier so often presented in official court chronicles.

Instead, we shall go back to his historical significance as a maker of the Muslim world. He is still considered in Moroccan textbooks as one of the main founding figures of Moroccan national history, a reputation enhanced by his keeping at bay Iberian and Ottoman interventionism, and by his uniting the country under a new series of administrative, economic and military measures that entailed the beginning of modernization. His administration, his dealings with the elites, his political discourse and most especially his ceremonial and celebrations (from *bay'a* to *Mawlid*) still form part of Moroccan dynastic power today. Somehow, the cultural foundations of Moroccan power can be traced back and explained by much of what al-Mansur did and established. In this respect he was successful and enduring. I have found the writing of this book very illuminating, for example, of some aspects of the power exercised by Hassan II, the father of the present King of Morocco.

There is one main issue that seems to me to be especially worthy of underlining, even if it ended in failure. That is Ahmad al-Mansur's obsession with America. Al-Mansur was aware of the potentially strong role of Morocco in the Atlantic and strove to fulfil it; in this he also was a precursor and a 'maker'. He had bought into the notion that the American theatre was where the future of the mighty nations of his time would be played out, nations that we now perceive as being on the brink of modernity. Al-Mansur's obsession with America shows at least a great political perspicacity, and at most an extraordinary level of intelligence and an ability to see into the future.

Al-Mansur did everything he possibly could to take part in American schemes. We can be reasonably certain that it was his desire to take part in an American venture, for which he needed enough money to be admitted into the group of nations committed to missions of discovery and conquest, that led him to undertake the highly risky, and all but illegitimate, project to conquer Western Sudan. There is a fragile boundary between success and failure in large-scale ventures, and because his efforts led to failure al-Mansur's ambitions now seem totally off the mark. But this was certainly not the view of his contemporaries – not of the Englishmen who recommended an alliance with Morocco as a way of attacking Spanish territorial possessions in America, or indeed the Spaniards themselves, who saw the possible alliance as a very real threat that was often discussed and analysed at meetings of the State Council.

The notion of a Moroccan involvement in the Americas cropped up at other levels of Spanish society too. We saw that this possibility was one of the main reasons why captain Francisco de Aldana (mentioned in Chapter 1) gave his backing to Don Sebastian's invasion of Morocco. In the late 1580s, during the crisis following the failure of the Invincible Armada, the famous visionary Lucrecia de León – who had a great following among the people, but who was also influential at the Spanish court – predicted the fall of the Habsburg Empire, to be brought about by the arrival of the Muslims in America in connivance with the English: Drake and the Turk, as she put it. The fact that none of this ever occurred – neither the Ottomans nor the Moroccans played any role in the division of American spoils in terms of territory or trade – is, in my view, a decisive factor in the relegation of the Mediterranean Islamic world to the margins of modernity.

Among conclusions we now also have to consider the almost fatally weak political structure of al-Mansur's Morocco. It was a country characterized by a lack of internal social cohesion as well as by concerns about the legitimacy of the sultan's power, as we have seen in the excessive amount of messianic rhetoric employed by his regime.

Diverse factors contributed to this situation: the ambiguous split in nominal authority between Sufi *shaykhs* and the *'ulama*, with the associated debates and struggles for moral authority and definition of the community; the importance of the *shurafa* (the descendants of the Prophet) as a tangible and permanent manifestation of the Prophet in Morocco, a kind of 'mystical body'. On the other hand were the divisions of the population into local and tribal communities inland and, on the coast, Moriscos, corsairs, foreign merchants and Renegades. During the reign of Ahmad al-Mansur, the presence of the Moriscos, usually regarded by historians as representing a positive contribution in both demographic and cultural terms, seems to have been a disruptive factor or even a hazardous and potentially explosive ingredient that needed to be handled carefully, both internally and in terms of foreign policy decisions.

To overcome these divisions, al-Mansur employed different means at different levels, beginning and ending with force to compel obedience and inculcate fear. At the political level was the manner in which different elite groups had access to centres of power and in particular to the *Dar al-makhzen*, the sovereign's inner circle, through service, personal friendships and the exchange of gifts and favours. Such friendships and gift exchange forced the elites to engage in rivalries and dispute. Other, smaller power centres, such as the minor courts of al-Mansur's sons in their respective governorships, employed the same practices. In a society fractured by multiple internal cleavages, the sultan was the supreme arbiter, and he derived his power from that arbitration; there can be little doubt, then, that he saw a need to maintain and even create these internal divisions. The use of harsh symbolic and physical violence on his subjects also played a key role in Ahmad al-Mansur's execution of power.

Sufi lodges and their networks, disciplined groups of initiates, religious scholars and *shurafa,* fortresses, palaces for military governors and royal processions: all formed part of the visualization and practice of power in sixteenth-century Morocco, and they have continued to play a role into post-Independence days. Above that was theatrical display, pageantry and ceremony, centred upon the stage-set constructed at Marrakesh. All were then embraced by the grandiose claim to caliphate and the sultan's messianic role as the *Mahdi* to bring about 'the end of history'. All, however, were subject to the fundamental weakness of the sultan's mortality.

Structural weakness and a lack of internal cohesion meant that the country was unable to withstand a crisis, such as that which arises at the death of the sovereign; when a king died, the whole social and political edifice constructed during his reign collapsed. In the case of al-Mansur, the symptoms of collapse were manifest even before the end of his life. Rising prices, starvation and the plague certainly did not help, but externally there was a change of scene. Philip II signed the Vervins peace treaty with France in 1598, and died at the end of that same year. His successor, Philip III, made peace with James I of England in 1604 and with the Dutch in 1609. The confrontation between the two halves of Europe that Ahmad al-Mansur had used profitably suddenly disappeared. An opportunity had passed, and the displacement of power towards the north of Europe would mean that the country that Ahmad al-Mansur had tried to bring to the centre of world influence would remain for ever on the periphery.

SOURCES AND
BIBLIOGRAPHY

There is a wide range of sources for the study of Ahmad al-Mansur's reign, written in Arabic, Portuguese and Spanish, Jewish Arabic and Hebrew, and English. In fact, there is a great deal more primary material than secondary. Here I have noted the most important texts from which I have drawn.

WORKS BY AL-MANSUR'S COURTIERS AND SECRETARIES

Al-Fishtali, *Manahil al-safa'*, ed. A. Karim. Rabat, 1973

Al-Ifrani, *Nuzhat al-hadi fi akhbar muluk al-qarn al-hadi*, Arabic edition and French translation by O. Houdas, Paris, 1889

Al-Tamagruti, *Kitab al-nafha al-miskiyya fi-l-sifara al-turikiyya*, ed. Lith. Fez (n.d.), French translation by H. de Castries, Paris, 1929

Ibn al-Qadi, *Al-Muntaqa l-maqsur 'ala ma'athir al-khalifa al-Mansur*, ed. M. Razzuq, Rabat, 1986

There is no such thing as archives and archival documents in Morocco for this period of Moroccan history. The reasons for the lack of an 'archival mind' in this context are numerous and much discussed by scholars. In the Moroccan context, elites found other ways of establishing records of their right to privileges, including genealogical texts in *sharif* families, dictionaries of *'ulama* and hagiographic repertoires of saints. The most important of these are:

Ahmad Baba, *Nayl al-Ibtihaj*, in the margins of Ibn Farhun, *Dibaj*, Beirut (n.d.)

Al-Badisi, *Al-maqsad al-sharif wa-l-manzi' al-latif*, Rabat, 1982

Al-Fasi, *Mumti' al-asma' fi akhbar al-Jazuli wa-l-Tabba' wa-ma lahuma min al-atba'*, Fez, 1887

Ibn al-Ahmar, *Buyutat Fas al-kubra*, Rabat, 1972

Al-Manjur, *Fihris Ahmad al-Manjur*, ed. M. Hajji, Rabat, 1976

Al-Tadili, *Al-Tashawwuf ila rijal al-tasawwuf*, ed. A. Toufiq, Rabat, 1984

Al-Hajari, the Andalusian translator and secretary, wrote a book about his trip to Europe that has been edited and translated into English: P. S. Van Koningsveld, Q. Al-Samarrai and G. Wiegers, *Kitab nasir al-Din 'ala l-qawm al-Kafirin* (*The Supporter of Religion against the Infidel*), Madrid, 1997.

The most important Jewish Moroccan chronicles were published and translated by Georges Vajda in his book *Un recueil de textes historiques judéo-marocaines*, Paris, 1951.

The Sudanese chronicle I consulted for Chapter 6 is Al-Sa'di, *Tarikh al-Sudan*, ed. and trans. O. Houdas, Paris, 1898–1900. This is the text where the order 'Corten le la cabeza' appears. The Spanish anonymous 'Relación de la jornada que el Rey de Marruecos ha hecho de la conquista del Reyno de Gago', also used in Chapter 6, was published by H. de Castries in the journal *Hespéris*, 3 (1923), 433–88.

ARCHIVAL DOCUMENTS

Much archival material, including documents such as treaties and letters from al-Mansur's chancellery, is preserved in European archives. The French scholars Henry de Castries and Pierre de Cenival launched a monumental series entitled *Les Sources Inédites de l'Histoire du Maroc* (SIHM) at the Institut d'Etudes Marocaines in Rabat under the French Protectorate, which ran from 1904 until the early 1960s. They published documents from and about Morocco which survive in European collections, dividing the material among the volumes according to the country where the documents are preserved. I have made abundant use of the volumes containing documents from Portugal, England and the Low Countries. The SIHM volumes containing documentation from Spain go to 1575, before the battle of Alcazar, and those of Portugal, to immediately after. The narratives about the battle of Alcazar used in this book (such as those by Fray Luis Nieto or Conestaggio) are included in the first volume of the SIHM dedicated to France (*France*, Ière série vol. 1). Another volume of Moroccan documents found in Spanish archives covers the period of the lives of al-Mansur and his sons: it has been edited (with an introduction) by M. García-Arenal, F. R. Mediano and R. El Hour, *Cartas marruecas. Documentos de Marruecos en archivos españoles (siglos XVI–XVII)*, Madrid, 2002.

The letters of Juan de Silva, Spanish ambassador to Lisbon, and Philip II used for Chapter 1 on the battle of Alcazar are published in Volume 5 of the *Colección de Documentos Inéditos para la Historia de España* (CODOIN), Madrid, 1842–95. This volume includes different narratives by witnesses of Alcazar. There is also a good deal of Portuguese documentation written by captives of Alcazar or by officials of the Portuguese Moroccan ports. The ones used most often and drawn upon here are Jeronimo de Mendoça, *Jornada de Africa*, Lisbon, 1607, and Antonio de Saldanha, *Cronica de Almançor, sultão de Marrocos*, ed. A. Dias Farinha, Lisbon, 1997. The description of the wealthy Jewish merchant who arrived in Oran with a cargo of sugar is in Diego Suárez Montañés, *Historia del Maestre último que fue de Montesa*, ed. M. Bunes and B. Alonso, Valencia, 2004. Much information about the army and administration is to be gathered from Diego de Torres, *Relación del origen y suceso de los Xarifes y de los reinos de Marruecos, Fez y Tarudante*, Seville, 1581, ed. M. García-Arenal, Madrid, 1980.

Many years of research in the Archivo General de Simancas (Valladolid) and the Archivo Ducal de Medinasidonia (Sanlúcar de Barrameda, Cadiz) form part of my personal experience with the sources upon which part of this book is based. My work on the Inquisition records of Jews, Moriscos and Renegades kept at the Archivo Histórico Nacional in Madrid has also been part of the background of this study. The Tribunal of Granada contains important records of Moriscos whose trial was carried out in absentia, the crime of the culprits being to have fled to the Maghreb, evidence of their retention of their Islamic faith.

BIBLIOGRAPHY

Most studies of Ahmad al-Mansur are in French and Spanish. Among the most important titles are the works of French scholars written during the Protectorate or soon after, such as G. Deverdun, *Marrakech des origines à 1912*, Rabat, 1959 (a classic); P. Berthier, *Les anciennes sucreries au Maroc et leur réseau hydraulique*, Rabat, 1966; Gabriel Rousseau, *Le mausolée des princes sa'-diens à Marrakech*, Paris, 1925; R. Ricard, *Études sur l'histoire des Portugais au Maroc*, Coimbra, 1955. In Spanish I recommend the wonderful Jaime Oliver Asín, *Vida de don Felipe de Africa, príncipe de Fez y de Marruecos*, Madrid, 1955.

More recent titles, and in English, include Dahiru Yahya, *Morocco in the Sixteenth Century. Problems and Patterns in African Foreign Policy*, London,

1981, which is a bit outdated. A richer text is Andrew Hess, *The Forgotten Frontier. A History of the Sixteenth-Century Ibero-African Frontier*, Chicago and London, 1978, which focuses on the Ottomans and the Spaniards, Morocco being marginal to the book. That is also the problem, from our point of view, of Fernand Braudel's monumental work on the Mediterranean world in the times of Philip II; it practically leaves Morocco out, but it is illuminating for context, corsairs, Renegades, Moriscos, etc. On Moriscos, the most recent book in English is L. P. Harvey, *Muslims in Spain (1500 to 1614)*, Chicago and London, 2005, which also discusses Moriscos in Morocco and in the conquest of Sudan. It is a book worth reading. On the battle of Alcazar: Lucette Valensi, *Fables de la Mémoire. La glorieuse bataille des trois rois*, Paris, 1992, translated into Arabic and Portuguese. The most accessible account of the conquest of Timbuktu in English is E. W. Bovill, *The Golden Trade of the Moors*, 2nd edition, ed. Robin Hallet, London, 1968. On the army, Weston Cook, *The Hundred Years War for Morocco: Gunpowder and the Military Revolution in the Early Modern Muslim World*, Boulder, 1994.

On Sufi brotherhoods and their political role are Vincent Cornell, *Realm of the Saint. Power and Authority in Moroccan Sufism*, Austin, 1998, and Abdellah Hammoudi, *Master and Disciple. The cultural Foundations of Moroccan Authoritarianism*, Chicago and London, 1999. The work of two famous anthropologists, Ernst Gellner, *Saint of the Atlas*, London, 1969, and Clifford Geertz, *Islam Observed. Religious development in Morocco and Indonesia*, New York, 1968, are relevant for the discussion of issues considered in this book. In the Conclusion, I have referred to King Hassan II as presented by the historian Abdallah Laroui, *Le Maroc et Hassan II. Un témoignage*, Quebec and Casablanca, 2005; Spanish translation, *Marruecos y Hassan II. Un testimonio*, Madrid, 2007.

I have of course made use of my own books *Messianism and Puritanical Reform: Mahdis of the Muslim West*, Leiden, Brill, 2006, and, with G. Wiegers, *A Man of Three Worlds. Samuel Pallache, a Moroccan Jew in Catholic and Protestant Europe*, Baltimore, Johns Hopkins University Press, 2003 (English translation of *Un hombre en tres mundos: Samuel Pallache, un judío marroquí entre la Europa protestante y la católica*, Madrid, Siglo XXI, 2nd edition 2007).

SELECTION OF ARTICLES

Aimes, G., 'Le palais d'El-Bedi, à Marrakech et le mausolée des Chorfas Saadiens', *Archives Berbères* 3 (1918), 53–64

Cornell, V. J., 'Socioeconomic Dimensions of Reconquista and Jihad in Morocco: Portuguese Dukkala and Sa'did Sus', *International Journal of Middle East Studies* 22 (1990), 379–418

Dakhlia, J., 'Dans la mouvance du prince: la symbolique du pouvoir itinérant au Maghreb', *Annales. Économies, Sociétés, Civilisations* 43 (1988), 735–60

Elboudrari, H., 'Quand les saints font les villes: lecture anthropologique de la pratique sociale d'un saint marocain du XVIIᵉ siècle', *Annales. Économies, Sociétés, Civilisations* 3 (1985), 489–508

Fleischer, C. H., 'The Lawgiver as Messiah: the Making of the Imperial Image in the Reign of Süleymân', in G. Venstein (ed.), *Soliman le Magnifique et son Temps*, Paris, 1992, 159–77

García-Arenal, M., 'Los andalusíes en el ejército sa'dí: un intento de golpe de estado contra Ahmad al-Mansur (1978)', *Al-Qantara*, 5 (1984), 169–202

——, '*Mahdi*, Murabit, Sharif: l'avènement de la dynastie sa'dienne', *Studia Islamica* 70 (1990), 77–114

——, 'Sainteté et pouvoir dynastique au Maroc: la résistance de Fès aux Sa'diens', *Annales. Économies, Sociétés, Civilisations* 4 (1990), 1019–42

Hunwick, J. O., 'Songhay, Bornu and Hausaland in the Sixteenth Century', in *The Cambridge History of Africa*, London, 1974

——, 'Ahmad Baba and the Moroccan Invasion of the Sudan (1591)', *Journal of the Historical Society of Nigeria* 2 (1962), 311–28

Jacques-Meunié, D., 'Le grand Riad du Palais du Badi' selon le plan publié par Windus', *Hespéris* 44 (1957), 129–34

Moudden, A. El, 'The idea of the Caliphate between Moroccans and Ottomans: Political and Symbolical Stakes in the 16th and 17th Century Maghrib', *Studia Islamica* 82 (1995), 103–12

Necipoglu, G., 'Süleyman the Magnificent and the Representation of Power in the Context of Ottoman–Hapsburg–Papal Rivalry', *Art Bulletin* 71 (1989), 401–27

Rodríguez Mediano, F., 'Justice, crime et châtiment au Maroc au 16e siècle', *Annales HSS,* May–June (1996), 3, 611–27

——, 'L'amour, la justice et la crainte dans les récits hagiographiques marocains', *Studia Islamica* 90 (2000), 85–104

——, 'Le regard qui pénètre le monde : pouvoir et sacralité au Maroc (XVI et XVII siècles', *Al-Qantara*, 17 (1996), 473–87

Rosenberger, B., Triki, H., 'Famines et épidémies au Maroc aux XVIᵉ–XVIIᵉ siècles', *Hespéris-Tamuda* 14 (1973), 109–75

Sebti, A., 'Au Maroc: sharifisme citadin, charisme et historiographie', *Annales. Économie, Sociétés, Civilisations* 41 (1986), 433–57

——, 'Présence des crises dans la chronique dynastique marocaine: entre la narration et les signes', *Cahiers d'Études Africaines* 30, 119 (1990), 237–50

Touati, H. 'L'arbre du Prophète. Prophétisme, ancestralité et politique au Maghreb', *Revue des Mondes Musulmans et de la Méditerranée* 91–4 (2000), 148–52

INDEX

Felipe of Africa *see* al-Shaykh, Muley
Ferdinand II, King of Aragon 62
Fez 43–4
  cultural and intellectual centre 72
  Jewish population 70
  Mellah of 70–1
firearms 56, 80–1
al-Fishtali 37
fitna 122–3
France 131, 143

Gasparo Corso, Andrea 27, 30
Gasparo Corso, Francisco 27
generosity 121–2
al-Ghazwani 114
gold 74, 98–9, 103, 107
Granada, fall of 18, 62
Granville, Richard 82
guish tribes 55, 56
Guyana (Venezuela) 95–6

hadiths 128
al-Hajari 67–8
al-Hajj Massa 34
Hassan II, King of Morocco 140
Hassan Pasha 28
Henrique, Cardinal Don 7, 12, 77
Hogan, Edmund 26–7, 30
Holland
  colonies 96
  eastern trade 93
  peace with 143
  relations with Morocco 87–8
horses 33
al-Humaydi, Abdelwahid 112–13

Iberian union 7, 76
  consequences of 82–7
Ibn Battuta 98
Ibn Qarqush 112
al-Ifrani 30, 36, 112, 121, 128–9
ilj, the 60
infantes moros, los 84–5
Inquisition, the 62
  in Portugal 69–70
Invincible Armada 83
Isabella I, Queen of Castile 62
Islam
  converts to 60–1

  providential role of 69
Isma'il al-Safavi 132–3
Isma'il, Muley 25, 77, 85, 119, 136

Jahiliyya 122–3
James I, King of England 143
jaysh tribes 55
al-Jazuli 114
Jazuliyya 52, 53, 114, 124–5
  rebellion 112
Jews
  expertise 72–3
  name used as insult 16
  in Portugal 69
  in Spain 62, 68–9
jihad 123
  see also Sudan
João III, King of Portugal 69–70
judería see Mellah of Fez
judiciary 58

khadim al-haramayn al-sharifayn 131–2
Khayzuran 38, 136
Kitab al-Tadhkira (al-Qurtubi) 130

Lane, Augustine 33
Lane, Ralph 33
Larache 10, 78, 137
Leo Africanus 69, 98, 100
León, Lucrecia 141
Lepanto, battle of 28–9
Levant Company 81
Lewis, Bernard 1
Lyautey, General 131

Madoc, Lawrence 108
madrasas 48
Mahdi, the 123, 124–5
  and Ahmad al-Mansur 128–32
Mahmud Zarqun 107
al-makhzaniya 55
Manoel I, King of Portugal 69
Mansa Musa 99
Mansorico (Mansur Abd al-Rahman) 107
Mansur Abd al-Rahman (Mansorico) 107
manuscripts 98
al-Manzari, Ali 45
Maqil Arabs 56
Marinid dynasty 43, 48, 70–2